MEETINGS WITH PASTERNAK

MEETINGS WITH PASTERNAK

A Memoir by
Alexander Gladkov

---

*Translated from the Russian
and edited with notes and introduction by*
Max Hayward

A Helen and Kurt Wolff Book
Harcourt Brace Jovanovich
New York and London

Published in Russian under the title *Vstrechi s Pasternakom* by YMCA Press,
Paris, 1973

ISBN 0-15-158590-3

First American Edition

B C D E

CONTENTS

INTRODUCTION

"Like rafts down a river, like a convoy of barges,
The centuries will float to me out of the darkness.
And I shall judge them."

The present work is the first important memoir of Pasternak to have emerged so far from the Soviet Union, where it has been in limited circulation as a *samizdat* manuscript for several years.† It was published in Russian in Paris in 1973.

Alexander Gladkov, who died in Moscow in 1976, was a playwright at one time associated with Meyerhold's theatre. He is best known for a play in verse, *Long, Long Ago*, about Napoleon's invasion of Russia, which had its première in Leningrad in 1941.

As he describes at the beginning, Gladkov first met Pasternak in Meyerhold's apartment in 1936. After this they saw each other only fleetingly until the war years, when they both lived for several months in the small town of Chistopol on the river Kama (November 1941 – March 1942). Pasternak, together with many leading Soviet writers, was evacuated here during the German threat to Moscow in the autumn of 1941, and in this comparatively relaxed provincial environment he often talked to Gladkov at length, sharing his inner reflections with him in a way which, even for someone so unusually trusting and spontaneous, would have seemed unthinkable in the capital city.

Gladkov recorded their conversations in a diary he kept at the time. Their contact continued, more intermittently, during the remaining years of the war, after both returned to Moscow in 1942. In several meetings after the war, Pasternak again showed a remarkable degree of confidence in Gladkov, speaking his mind about the state of affairs in the country with astonishing frankness. Gladkov provides the first direct testimony that *Doctor Zhivago*, which Pasternak began writing in 1946, was deliberately

† It is referred to in Nadezhda Mandelstam's *Hope Abandoned*, and there is even a brief quotation from it in the discussion of Pasternak in the *History of Soviet Russian Literature* published by the Academy of Sciences of the USSR (Vol. 3, 1969).

conceived as a challenge to everything Stalin and his régime stood for.

In 1948 Gladkov, like countless other Soviet intellectuals in those years, was arrested and sent to a forced labour camp, from which he was released only after Stalin's death. He now again met Pasternak on a number of occasions, and gives a vivid idea of his mood during the campaign of persecution launched against him after *Doctor Zhivago* had been published abroad in 1957. The memoir ends with an account of Pasternak's funeral in June 1960, when in death, as he had sometimes done in life, he brought together a large number of his fellow countrymen for whom he represented a unique "repository of other values" – to quote the words of one of the poets of the younger generation influenced by him.

One of the most important aspects of Gladkov's memoir is that, through his account of the part played by Pasternak in his own intellectual and spiritual development, he conveys a sense of what the poet meant for Russia as a whole, of the way in which a man who seemed childishly innocent and ineffectual in his practical dealings not only withstood, almost alone, the intolerable pressures of the times, but also came to be seen by many as a last surviving focus of moral resistance to the infinitely cruel and merciless master of the country's destiny. It is still not easy to explain why Stalin should have spared Pasternak when so many others were done to death, imprisoned, or reduced to abject silence for much less. There was a conscious, if for the most part unspoken, confrontation between the two. As we see from some passages in Gladkov's book, Pasternak was much preoccupied with his own attitude to Stalin – and Stalin clearly had the supreme tyrant's fascination for those very few poets and writers (Mandelstam, Pasternak, Bulgakov, Akhmatova) who could be destroyed but never completely bent to his will, whose genius, in his brutish way, he perceived and recognized.

Pasternak had always been thought of as an "ivory tower" figure remote from the immediate concerns of his age. The volumes of lyric poetry that first established his reputation, sometimes even by their titles – *Above the Barriers*, *My Sister Life* – marked him off as the antipode of a contemporary such as Mayakovski with his active involvement in the Revolution. Pasternak's principal themes – love, nature, life at its most everyday and ordinary – seemed to suggest that he was quite aloof from the great events taking place in the world. In the very

8

early days of the Revolution he pictured himself in a poem shouting through the window of his study to the children in the street: "What millennium is it out there?" – a line which has often been quoted as proof of his detachment from the history which was then in the making. His early verse (which in later life, somewhat unjustly, he tended to dismiss because of what he regarded as its abstruseness and lack of deeper content) is notable for its sheer exultation in the words themselves. With an unusually plastic language such as Russian it is easy enough for a poet of Pasternak's temperament to be carried away by the positively sensuous joy that comes from handling his material. He reminds one of a happy child marvelling at the world and his discovery of it, conveying his delight in a language which is as tangible a part of it as the sky, the trees, the snow and all the familiar objects of domestic life. For Pasternak nothing is so extraordinary as the ordinary, and he constantly tries to make us see it through his eyes by an exuberant use of metaphors of the kind quoted by Gladkov – raindrops are as weighty as cufflinks, and a branch of wet lilac blossom looks like a sparrow caught in a rainstorm. Many people, including Gladkov, have noted Pasternak's "self-centredness" and it was true in a literal sense: he stood at the centre of a perpetually astonishing universe, and his poetry is the tale of how, in all its diversity, it related to himself, the only fixed and immutable point. It was this "self-centredness", as much as his natural integrity, which made him impervious – though not indifferent – to the terrors and temptations of the age. From his unassailable vantage point he looked out at what was going on in the new millennium and found that most of it could not be assimilated to his poet's vision.

Like Osip Mandelstam, he was dominated by an inborn sense of "rightness" – the world could only be as he saw it, not as others might have wanted him to see it. Under a "normal" tyranny it would probably not have been difficult for Pasternak to have lived his life without much concern for the "history" he originally thought outside his province, but, like all his compatriots, he was confronted by a reality which forced itself on the attention with insistent, baleful malignance, demanding total subservience to itself, and never to be propitiated by mere acquiescence or tokens of compliance. The final human embodiment of this reality was, of course, Stalin. Since Pasternak could not accept it he was driven into a conflict which did violence to his nature by compelling him to take issue with a conception of the world

9

so warped and narrow that in the ordinary way of things it would have lain completely outside his field of vision. Whether he liked it or not, he eventually felt bound to respond to this aggressive "deutero-reality", which had intruded itself through the sheer force of its hostility, by putting it in the perspective of his own world – thereby showing what an alien and transient thing it was. To do this he had to depart from his habitual lyrical mode and adopt a form which came far less naturally to him – that of an extensive prose narrative (I shall return later to the problem of defining it). *Doctor Zhivago* was the result of Pasternak's determination to meet, in the only way he thought appropriate, a challenge which had to be answered as a matter of overriding duty – even though it conflicted, to some extent, with his beliefs about the nature of poetry and his own place in it. By the time of his first important conversations with Gladkov in the first few months of the war, Pasternak had already resolved to "speak out" if Stalin – as he evidently foresaw would be the case – began to rule even more harshly after victory over the Germans.

But in the earliest days of the Revolution Pasternak had been by no means totally unsympathetic towards it. He could not but be impressed by the grandiose sweep of events. His feelings at the time are reflected in a passage in *Doctor Zhivago* where his hero, Yuri, speaks of the atmosphere in the country after the fall of the monarchy in images which suggest that Pasternak saw no inevitable dichotomy between revolution and the eternal real world of nature and art he knew as a poet:

"Last night I was watching a meeting in the square . . . Mother Russia is on the move . . . she's talking and she can't stop. And it isn't as if only people were talking. Stars and trees meet and converse, flowers talk philosophy at night, stone houses hold meetings. It's like something out of the Gospels . . . The revolution broke out . . . like a breath that's been held too long. Everybody was revived, reborn, changed, transformed. You might say that everyone has been through two revolutions – his own personal revolution as well as the general one. It seems to me that socialism is the sea, and all these separate streams, these private individual revolutions are flowing into it – the sea of life, of life in its own right. I said life, but I mean life as you see it in a work of art, transformed by genius, creatively enriched."

Even Lenin's usurpation of the revolution had its momentary appeal for Yuri Zhivago – and hence, we may infer, for Pasternak:

"Such a huge event cannot be asked for its credentials, it has no need to give dramatic proof of its existence, we'll take it on trust. It would be mean and petty to try to dig for the causes of titanic happenings." In 1921 Pasternak saw Lenin in the flesh as he spoke at the 9th Congress of Soviets in the Bolshoi Theatre, and evidently recognized him as a genius indeed capable of transforming life, but when he described the occasion in a poem written towards the end of the twenties (not long before Stalin finally established himself in supreme power), it was in full and prophetic consciousness of the tragic fate of all revolutionary beginnings: "A genius comes as a harbinger of betterment, and his going is avenged with tyranny."

It is apparent from this, and from much else he wrote during the first decade and a half after the Revolution that Pasternak's reputation as an "ivory tower poet" was in fact quite undeserved, and that his professed ignorance of what millennium he was living in could only be understood in an ironical sense. Although nature is the dominating theme of his lyric poetry, he frequently shows his acute awareness of history as the other dimension of human existence. As Andrei Sinyavski has pointed out,† already well before the Revolution Pasternak had arrived at a precise, almost schematic notion of the relationship between nature and history which remained with him, in one form or another, to the end of life and was at the centre of his understanding of his own position as a poet. In *The Black Goblet*, an essay published in 1916, Pasternak distinguished between "eternity" and "time" as separate spheres of being. Our lives run their course in "time", which we experience as "history" – the arena of "heroes" or "men of action". Transcending and enfolding it, as a not directly knowable category, "eternity" is the concern of the lyric poet, who enables us to glimpse it fleetingly in nature and art. The poet, as the temporal representative of "eternity" is thus always the antithesis of those who "make history". In Russia, ever since the days of Pushkin and Nicholas I, the opposition of poet and tsar has seemed particularly stark and tragic, a drama always awaiting re-enactment, and forty years after writing *The Black Goblet*, Pasternak had more than theoretical reasons to revert to the same language in defining his role as a poet:

†In his introductory article – a miracle of suggestiveness, considering the circumstances in which it was written – to Pasternak's *Poems* (Moscow, 1965). See also Olga Hughes: *The Poetic World of Boris Pasternak*, Princeton, 1974.

Poet, keep watch, keep watch,
You must not fall asleep –
You are eternity's hostage
In captivity to time.

Throughout history absolute rulers have sometimes felt a certain awe before poets and philosophers – the "hostages of eternity" defenceless in the face of their temporal might. In the case of Stalin, the word "awe" would be misplaced, but he undoubtedly had a kind of superstitious appreciation of the supreme worth of those very few who in every generation stand outside and above their age. It is significant that, with the exception of Osip Mandelstam, none of the indisputably great writers who had been recognized as such before Stalin's assumption of supreme power were killed or even imprisoned by him – although he knew very well how inimical they were to him by their very nature. Hosts of lesser writers – including some distinguished by little else but their expressions of dog-like devotion to the new order – were swept away in successive waves of terror, quite indiscriminately, with casual contempt. The case of Mandelstam was anomalous. The miracle is that he was not summarily executed in 1934 for the poem in which, in words shorn of any allegorical circumlocution, he described Stalin as a murderer surrounded by braying and whinnying "half-men". In an unprecedented and never subsequently repeated act of clemency, after Bukharin, Akhmatova and Pasternak had pleaded for his life, Stalin contented himself with having Mandelstam exiled to a provincial town. In the circumstances it was a fate not much worse than what had befallen Ovid or Pushkin. When Mandelstam returned to Moscow in 1937, it was at the height of the Great Terror, and it is scarcely to be wondered at that someone who had committed such blatant *lèse-majesté* only three years previously should now have been re-arrested – to die, this time, on the way to a concentration camp. It may be that Mandelstam's second arrest was the result of direct orders from Stalin, but it could equally well have been owing to a zealous initiative at a lower level – such initiatives were not lacking in those days, when Stalin himself could hardly have concerned himself with one individual among the vast numbers being rounded up. But, on the other hand, when the death of Mandelstam came to his attention, it could possibly have occasioned a slight displeasure: this much we may judge from the rumours, reported by Nadezhda

12

Mandelstam in her memoirs, that the end of Mandelstam was quoted in high official circles in 1939 as an example of the "excesses" committed by Yezhov. It is not inconceivable that Pasternak's survival during the post-war years, when – as Gladkov and others clearly show – he made no secret of his intention to speak his mind, was due to Stalin's unwillingness to see the case of Mandelstam repeated. If this is so, then it may not be fanciful to believe that Pasternak's dossier bore some specific indication that he was not to be touched without permission from Stalin himself.

Although they were physically spared, neither Pasternak nor Akhmatova went unmolested in the years after the war. In both cases (apart from odious campaigns of abuse in the press), attempts were made to break them by the persecution of people dear to them. With Akhmatova a partial success was achieved: her son, Lev Gumilev, was arrested (not for the first time) in 1949 and sent to a camp, and a year later – obviously in the hope of obtaining clemency for him – she published several poems in praise of Stalin. But when applied to Pasternak, this same tactic failed. In 1946, as Gladkov reports, "a great new love entered his life". This was Olga Vsevolodovna Ivinskaya, a literary editor and translator then in her mid-thirties, who became Pasternak's companion and was with him till the end of his life. She managed his practical affairs, collaborated on translations with him, and provided the inspiration for Lara, the heroine of *Doctor Zhivago*. In 1949 she was arrested, held in the Lubianka, and sentenced to five years in a forced labour camp – from which she was released after Stalin's death. As one can judge from several of the poems (such as "Parting") in the *Zhivago* cycle devoted to her, Pasternak was infinitely distressed by this cruel blow. But it did not have the desired result. He made no concessions and went on writing the book in which, as no one had ever done before, he was to settle accounts with the epoch through which he had lived.

It could be that Stalin spared Pasternak himself for no other reason than that he hoped eventually to exact a poetic tribute from him as well. This would obviously have been of triple advantage, as he no doubt calculated in his cynical fashion: he would be "immortalized" by a real genius, the rebel poet would be punished far more excruciatingly than by death or imprisonment, and the many Russian intellectuals who, cowed and demoralized as they were, still looked to Pasternak with secret

13

hope ("Everything changes under our zodiac, only Pasternak remains Pasternak", as the saying then went) would finally despair and inwardly submit if this last bastion fell.

Perhaps, however, it was not quite as simple as this. There is slight evidence of a special element of some kind in the relationship between Stalin and Pasternak. Nothing else can explain the extraordinary immunity enjoyed by Pasternak between 1946 and 1953, when on various occasions he read chapters of *Doctor Zhivago* to small private gatherings, and even lent parts of the manuscript to a number of people. In 1948, as Gladkov tells us, he read the opening poem of the *Zhivago* cycle, "Hamlet", with its clear declaration of his intention to "speak out", to a group of actors at one of the Moscow theatres. All this, needless to say, provided a rich harvest for the secret police. It is known that the then head of the Ministry of State Security, Abakumov, took a personal interest in Pasternak, and that a "case" was ready on the basis of which he could at any moment have been arrested and charged as a "British agent" (it was, of course, enough that his two sisters lived in Oxford). There can be little doubt, therefore, that he can only have survived in those years (not to mention his equally miraculous survival in 1937) because he was under Stalin's personal "protection".

It might be thought that, in general terms, Pasternak enjoyed a peculiar kind of "fool's licence". His extreme spontaneity, the almost child-like directness and lack of guile so vividly described by Gladkov, could possibly have impressed the morbidly suspicious Stalin more than all the protestations of loyalty he was so used to hearing – and of which, like any despot, he knew the true worth. But this can scarcely be the whole explanation. The most plausible single reason was suggested some years ago in a remarkable article published in a Russian-language journal in New York by an emigré writer and ex-Red Army officer, Mikhail Koriakov.† Koriakov draws attention to a highly unusual circumstance connected with the death of Stalin's second wife, Nadezhda Alliluyeva, in November 1932. There were many rumours about this at the time – according to some, Stalin had murdered her. The truth appears to be that she shot herself, probably in a fit of depression over the terrible consequences of collectivization, or as a protest against it. The official version was that she had died of peritonitis. If Stalin ever showed himself capable of normal human feelings, it was probably only in his relations with

† *The New Review*, New York, 1958

14

Alliluyeva. There is at any rate a good deal of evidence (in his daughter's memoirs, for instance) that he was shattered and grief-stricken by her death. It also seems certain that the pathological side of his nature was accentuated by this tragedy in his personal life. The frenzied paranoia that overwhelmed him in 1937, and then again in the post-war years – culminating in the violent anti-Semitic paroxysm of the "Doctors' Plot" – may easily have had its roots here. The "cult" of his personality was already then well under way, and the announcement of Alliluyeva's death was naturally followed by fulsome and stereotyped expressions of condolence from leading representatives of various professional and other bodies. A letter to Stalin from the Union of Writers was published in *Literary Gazette* of November 19, 1932. It was signed by thirty-three people (of whom six were liquidated a few years later), and was as trite in style as it was manifestly insincere in sentiment: ". . . Accept our grief at the death of N. S. Alliluyeva who devoted all her strength to the cause of the liberation of the millions of oppressed humanity, the cause which is headed by you, and for which we are ready to sacrifice our lives in confirmation of its unbreakable, life-giving force."

Pasternak evidently refused to sign this letter, since it is followed by a brief separate message from him which is astonishing both for its laconic, almost casual manner, and for what it says: "I share the feelings of the comrades. The day before [the announcement of Alliluyeva's death] I thought deeply and intensively about Stalin; as a poet – for the first time. Next morning I read the news. I was shaken, as though I had been there, living by his side, and had seen it. Boris Pasternak." It is impossible to convey the quality of the original in translation. There is an absolute minimum of words – pronouns and auxiliary parts of speech are left out, as in a telegram. Yet – perhaps because of this, and the total lack of sycophancy – it creates an impression of genuine compassion. To anyone familiar with the stylized manner of such pronouncements in the Soviet press, even in those early days of the "cult of personality", it will seem well nigh incredible that something as eccentric as this could have appeared in print. Quite apart from the pointed gesture of dissociation from the other "comrades", there is an almost sacrilegious note in the phrase about having thought of Stalin "for the first time". And why "as a poet"? Most extraordinary of all is the suggestion that Pasternak had a premonition of Alliluyeva's death – a hint of "mysticism" surely unparalleled in a context of such a kind. Koriakov believes that it was this which must somehow have awakened in Stalin a superstitious feeling that Pasternak, as a poet, was gifted with second sight. It is hard to say whether this was literally so, but one may readily agree with Koriakov's claim to have found here an important clue to the mystery of Pasternak's survival in later years. Such an oddly phrased message from Pasternak must have caught Stalin's eye at this critical moment in his personal life, marking him off from other men in a way that, for whatever unfathomable motives, prompted Stalin to grant him the kind of protection enjoyed by almost no one else.

This strange incident was the beginning of an obscure and distant, but none the less definable relationship between the two, the main stages of which may be clearly traced, at least on Pasternak's side. Almost two years later, in July 1934, it was followed by the famous telephone call from Stalin to Pasternak which has been described by Akhmatova and Nadezhda Mandelstam.† Stalin's purpose was to let it be known that he had heeded Pasternak's and Akhmatova's pleas on behalf of Mandelstam, which had been conveyed to him by Bukharin, then editor of *Izvestia*. (Bukharin still retained a vestige of influence with Stalin, or at least had access to him, after his political defeat a few years earlier.) After an exchange about Mandelstam, Pasternak said he would like to meet Stalin and talk with him. "About what?" Stalin asked. "About life and death," Pasternak replied. At this point Stalin hung up. Pasternak's desperate and rather comic attempt to get back to Stalin via the Kremlin switchboard was fruitless, and for a long time afterwards he was deeply upset at what he regarded as his failure to make proper use of this unique opportunity of a personal contact with Stalin. It is clear that in his ingenuous and trusting way he felt he might somehow have been able to influence Stalin, to open his eyes to what was going on in the country. At that time, in the "breathing space" between collectivization and the horrors of 1937, Stalin seemed in some ways to be pursuing a more moderate policy, curbing the excesses of Marxist militancy in the cultural and other spheres – the aggressive "proletarian" writers' organization had been disbanded, and a more conventional approach to the teaching of Russian history had been introduced on Stalin's personal initiative. Most significant of all, no doubt, in Pasternak's eyes was that Stalin had listened to the voices of two poets and shown

†See *Hope Against Hope*, chapter 32.

16

mercy to a third who had mortally insulted him.

It is with this in mind that one must read an even more astounding "message" from Pasternak to Stalin which appeared on New Year's Day, 1936, in *Izvestia* – this time in verse, under the title "Two Poems". The last part of the second poem is clearly addressed to Stalin, though he is not actually mentioned by name. Superficially, it reads like a tribute to the Great Leader who lives behind the ancient Kremlin wall – not so much a man as the personification of "action on the whole globe's scale" – who has been appointed by fate to do what others before him had dreamed of, but had never dared put into effect. To some extent the poem is an expression of the hope, widespread among the intelligentsia in the mid-thirties, that Stalin might lead Russia back from revolutionary insanity into more traditional paths: one line notes pointedly that, while carrying out his "fabulous deeds", Stalin had kept the "old ways" intact, and "the centuries have grown as used to him" as they are to the chimes of the Kremlin's bells. This is a clear allusion to Stalin's seeming wish at that time to restore at least some of the outer forms of Russia's past, if not its substance. A whole stanza is devoted to emphasizing that, despite the vastness of what he was doing, this "genius of action" remained a human being. The image chosen to convey this is a very odd one – and indeed implicitly casts doubt on it. In what is perhaps a remarkable example of poetic intuition, if not of studied ambiguity, Pasternak tells us that when Stalin goes out hunting a hare, his gun echoes round the woods, "just like that of any man". This detail betrays an actual knowledge of Stalin's tastes – he was indeed fond of shooting. It is curious, however, that the blood-lust of the hunter – and in pursuit of such a frightened and defenceless quarry as a hare – should be alluded to as an illustration of Stalin's common humanity. It is hard not to see here a premonition of what was to happen only a little over a year after the poem was published. Even so, it was evidently written not without optimism and with some faith in the possibility of a kind of partnership ("a fugue for two voices") between the "extreme polarities" represented by the poet and the man of action. Pasternak was thus harking back in these lines to his old idea about the lyric poet and the "hero" belonging to utterly different spheres. Throughout the poem, there is an implication that the poet, though "infinitely small", can absorb the "genius of action" as he absorbs so many other things "like a sponge" – rather, perhaps, as "eternity" absorbs or swallows up "time". In the last line the poet proclaims his belief in the knowledge these two "extreme polarities" may have of each other, implying that if the "genius of action" heeds the voice of eternity (as Stalin had done, apparently, in pardoning Mandelstam), then all could be well even on the temporal plane.

It was a vain hope, soon to be rudely disappointed. Only Pasternak was capable of speaking to Stalin in this spirit. One wonders what Stalin made of the poem. Perhaps he was pleased to see himself described as a "genius of action". Bukharin would hardly have printed it in *Izvestia* if he had not been certain that it would be well received – he may have thought that Stalin would simply see in it an oblique expression of gratitude for the sparing of Mandelstam, but as an admirer of Pasternak's work he would also not have failed to appreciate the underlying meaning, which doubtless accorded well with his own pious hopes in those days.

The next few years showed the utter futility of imagining that Stalin could be "humanized". The great man-hunt of 1937-8 – one of the cruellest and most senseless of all times – resulted in the death or disappearance of many people close to Pasternak. He was terribly affected by the fate of the two Georgian poets Paolo Yashvili and Titian Tabidze, whom he had come to know during his first visit to Georgia in 1931, and he felt an almost personal responsibility for the hounding to death of Mandelstam in 1938, and the suicide of Marina Tsvetayeva in 1940 – this, in particular, preyed on his mind till the end of his life. Long after Stalin's death he expressed his feelings in a poem (one of the many still not published in the Soviet Union), of which Gladkov quotes the first lines:

> My soul, you are in mourning
> For all those close to me,
> Turned into a burial vault
> For all my martyred friends . . .

In the increasingly nightmarish atmosphere of the second half of the thirties Pasternak, like many others, found it harder and harder to write work of his own. His last volume of poetry (*Second Birth*) had been completed in 1931, and although he wrote a few poems in the mid-thirties, none – except the ones published in *Izvestia* – appeared in print until the collection *On Early Trains* came out in 1943. For most of the thirties he devoted himself almost exclusively to translation. In 1935 he published a volume of Georgian lyric poets, and his *Selected Translations* (of Kleist, Byron, Keats, Verlaine, Shakespeare, and others) appeared in 1940. In the same year he completed his translation of *Hamlet*. At the time of his meeting with Gladkov early in the war he was already working on *Romeo and Juliet*, which eventually came out, with other Shakespeare plays, in a two-volume edition in 1949. In the post-war years he did the first complete version of *Faust* to be published in the Soviet Union (1953), and also Schiller's *Maria Stuart*, which was produced on the stage in Moscow in 1957.

For many writers in those years, translation – and also writing for children – served as a refuge: it was a way of earning a living without the compromises or loss of integrity which the publication of original work increasingly entailed. But for Pasternak it had a much more positive significance. In many instances, he chose for translation works which said things he could no longer publicly express in his own name. In this respect his version of *Hamlet* was particularly important and must be seen almost as an essential prologue to *Doctor Zhivago*, which he started writing in earnest six or seven years later. Contrary to his temperament and his whole philosophy Pasternak, like Hamlet, found himself compelled by circumstances to respond, in whatever way lay open to him, to the outrages of which he was a witness, and which touched him so closely. As he makes plain in his essay on translating Shakespeare, he looked on Hamlet not as a weak and vacillating character but as a man who steeled himself to play a role alien to his nature. This view of himself as a tragic actor in the literal sense, forced despite himself to walk out on to the stage of history, was the subject of his poem "Hamlet" (probably written in 1946, when he began work on *Doctor Zhivago*):

> The noise is stilled. I come out on the stage . . .
> The darkness of the night is aimed at me
> Along the sights of a thousand opera glasses.
> Abba, Father, if it be possible,
> Let this cup pass from me . . .

The image of the opera glasses aimed at him out of the darkness aptly conveys the agonizing sense he had of being the focal point of a myriad obscure expectations among the many readers of his verse who looked to him, in mute hope, as the last person able to express, perhaps, what few even dared to think. In his conversations with Gladkov during and after the war, he spoke often of his feeling of being "in debt" to his readers – as he put it in a poem, it was "shameful to be a legend on all lips, and an empty name". In the later war years, when there seemed a slight prospect of easier times after victory, he was already casting around for a suitable way of speaking more directly to his readers than was possible in lyrical poetry or translations. His first attempt to do so took the form of an audacious narrative poem, a fragment of which was actually published in *Pravda* in October, 1943. Inevitably it was cut short and had to be abandoned, but it showed, in hardly veiled language, the startling lengths to which he was prepared to go once he had any opportunity of making himself heard.†

But with the renewal of the Terror against the intelligentsia in 1946, he was soon as effectively isolated from his readers as he had been before the war. Until 1949, when Ivinskaya was arrested, he got off comparatively lightly. There was no attempt to starve him into submission (as in the case of Akhmatova and Zoshchenko, who were expelled from the Union of Writers), and the worst that happened to him, as Gladkov describes, was the publication of a vicious attack by Alexei Surkov in the newspaper *Culture and Life* (March, 1947). He was able to continue work on his version of *Faust* – which, needless to say, he intended should speak as eloquently for himself as *Hamlet* had done. At the same time, assured of a livelihood by his contract for this and other translations, he wrote *Doctor Zhivago* – and courted arrest by reading parts of it to private gatherings.

During this period when most people, naturally enough, thought only of how to save their skins, Pasternak on one occasion showed his defiance in public, at a poetry reading in what was then the largest auditorium in Moscow, the Polytechnic Museum. Gladkov does not refer to it, which probably means that for some reason he was not present.†† It is worth describing at length, since it undoubtedly had enormous significance for the Moscow intelligentsia and for Pasternak himself. The event was announced several days beforehand, in January or February, 1948, in the newspaper *Evening Moscow* and was billed as "An Evening of

†The implications of this poem ("Nightglow") are discussed in my note on it, pages 192-4.
††I was then in Moscow as a member of the British Embassy, and had a seat in the front row. It was the only time I was able to see Pasternak.

Poetry on the theme: 'Down with the Warmongers! For a Lasting Peace and People's Democracy' " – this was already after the establishment of the Cominform and the beginning of the massive Soviet campaign against the "Aggressive North Atlantic Treaty". The score or more poets listed in the announcement as due to take part included Pasternak. This seemed doubly incredible: incredible that after recent attacks on him in the press he should have been invited by the organizers to attend, and even more incredible that he himself should have agreed to be associated with what was obviously going to be a crude manifestation of support for official propaganda. The immediate thought was that Pasternak might at last have succumbed to all the pressures, and was now going to be produced in public to demonstrate the fact. This, as soon appeared, was anything but the case, and it seems likely that he was invited only in the hope that he might avail himself of this chance of showing himself a "true Soviet poet" – and even if he failed to do this, his mere presence on such a platform, it was no doubt felt, would compromise him in the eyes of the many people who looked upon him as almost the last remaining poet who had not "fallen". An incidental calculation was, perhaps, that the appearance of his name in the list of participants would draw a much larger audience than could otherwise be expected to attend such undistinguished and predictable proceedings. It was only on this last point that the organizers were not disappointed. The large hall, often used for major propaganda lectures, was quite remarkably crowded: people were squatting on the steps in the aisles, and large numbers who had not been able to get tickets stood on the street outside, desperately hoping to buy one at the last moment. There was a perceptible air of excitement, most unusual for the apathetic Soviet audiences of those days.

About twenty poets trooped out on to the stage and sat down dutifully on chairs facing the audience. In front of them was a table, and a rostrum with a microphone. But Pasternak was not among them. One chair at the back of the stage remained empty. The tense expectancy in the hall gave way to what was quite evidently a mixture of disappointment and relief – after all, what would *he* have been doing in this company? It seemed probable that he had been excluded at the last moment, or had simply decided against it himself.

The reading was presided over by the novelist Boris Gorbatov, who took his seat at the table. He had a little bell in front of him.

The first poet summoned to come forward was Surkov. He stood at the rostrum and declaimed into the microphone some verse which went straight to the point, denouncing the North Atlantic Treaty, the warmongers and Churchill – who at that time was regarded as the prime mover in the Cold War because of the famous speech at Fulton in which he first used the phrase about an Iron Curtain between Eastern Europe and the West. As Surkov was halfway through his last line, the audience suddenly burst into loud applause and when he glanced over his shoulder, startled at this ovation which was so clearly not for him, he saw what everybody else could see: Pasternak had slipped in from the wings and was just taking his seat in the back row. He looked a little flustered, but was visibly very gratified as he made imploring gestures with his outstretched palms until the crowd eventually quietened down. The recital continued, with each of the successive poets delivering his rhymed invective in the accepted sub-Mayakovskian manner, perhaps uncomfortably aware of how out of place it now was, and grateful for the thin, impatient applause of the audience, which was restless and ill at ease. What could Pasternak possibly say that would have the slightest relevance to warmongers and the North Atlantic Treaty? At last Gorbatov called his name and motioned him towards the rostrum. The audience again went wild, clapping and shouting. As he advanced from his chair to the edge of the stage, he smiled rather shyly and again gestured with his hands as though begging people not to go too far in expressing their feelings about him.†

Instead of walking up to the microphone into which all the others had spoken, he came down some steps at the side of the stage and stood below, directly in front of the audience, shifting his feet slightly as he waited for the applause to die away. At last there was dead silence. He looked exactly as Gladkov describes him – extremely young, with a strikingly handsome face, on which there now appeared a rather mischievous, almost puckish, yet at the same time invincibly innocent expression. In his peculiarly nasal voice, drawing out the Russian vowels to at least twice their normal length, he said: "Unfortunately, I have no poems on the theme of the evening, but I will read you some

†He was well aware, as Mrs Mandelstam reports in *Hope Abandoned*, of what Stalin is supposed to have said when he heard of a similar reception in this same place for Akhmatova a few years previously (in 1944): "Who *organized* this standing ovation?"

things I wrote before the war." The tension was broken, and there was renewed applause. Beads of sweat appeared on Gorbatov's bald head.

Pasternak then recited several poems which were obviously known to the audience from his volumes of poetry published years before. After each of them there was tremendous applause. At one moment he forgot a line and was immediately prompted from various parts of the hall. People began to shout out requests for particular poems, and he was clearly ready to oblige, but things were getting out of hand, and Gorbatov looked more and more distressed − though he too was affected by the general mood, and at one point his lips could be seen moving as he followed the words of one of the poems. Somebody shouted *Shestdesiat shestoi davai!* ("Give us the Sixty-Sixth!") − this was a request for Pasternak's version of Shakespeare's sonnet which had been included in his volume of selected translations published in 1940. Perhaps it was fortunate that he did not recite these lines which so perfectly defined the general state of affairs, and his own situation in particular:

> . . . and art made tongue-tied by authority,
> And folly, doctor-like, controlling skill,
> And simple truth miscall'd simplicity,
> And captive good attending captain ill:
> Tir'd with all these, from these would I be gone,
> Save that, to die, I leave my love alone.†

The meeting was developing into an unheard-of public demonstration and Gorbatov started to ring his bell frantically, trying to bring the crowd to order. But for a long time the applause went on, and Pasternak stood there, smiling awkwardly and patently enjoying his dangerous triumph. At last Gorbatov managed to make himself heard and declared an intermission. (There were many empty seats during the second half of the programme. The only other noteworthy person on the platform was Ilya Ehrenburg who sat there listening sardonically. When his turn came, perhaps emboldened by Pasternak's example, he

† The 66th was one of only two Shakespeare sonnets selected by Pasternak for translation (the other was the 73rd), and his rendering is remarkably powerful and trenchant. A blander (but fairly close) version by Samuil Marshak appeared in a full collection of Shakespeare's sonnets which was awarded the Stalin Prize in 1949. (An interesting illustration of what a difference the context can make!)

said: "I must admit that I am more accustomed to cursing in prose, but I will read you some verse I wrote during the Spanish Civil War . . .")

Almost anybody but Pasternak would certainly have been arrested for such a "political provocation" – he had virtually sabotaged an important public meeting devoted to the "struggle for peace". His "immunity", however, still held good and, although the indirect sanctions against him continued to be relentless and cruel beyond words, he was not himself touched. Right until Stalin's death in 1953 he was able to go on writing the work which he considered to be of infinitely greater significance than anything he had written previously – and whose publication abroad in 1957 may be seen as the final stage in his relations with the dictator: a posthumous settling of accounts, an act of poetic justice in the literal sense.

When Gladkov read *Doctor Zhivago*, he was disappointed by it, and he devotes several pages of his memoir to explaining why. He is at pains to emphasize that what he says about it must be set against the background of his unbounded affection and respect for the author, and that his misgivings are based on purely aesthetic grounds: "As a gesture it is brave and heroic; its moral premises are impeccable. But the literary result is doubtful and a matter for debate."

Doctor Zhivago has, of course, never been the object of a genuine debate in Russia. If it is ever published there, it may one day receive the kind of critical appraisal that a work of literature can be given only in the course of free public discussion in its country of origin (as happened, for instance, in the case of Bulgakov's *The Master and Margarita*, a quarter of a century after it was written).† It is, of course, impossible to say what the result of a fair and dispassionate exchange of views would be in Russia. Some would presumably share Gladkov's opinion that Pasternak was attempting to write in a genre unsuited to him, and that – in form, at least – *Doctor Zhivago* therefore appears weakly derivative of the nineteenth-century Russian novel; others would certainly accept Pasternak's own view (which it will be easier to substantiate when the correspondence of his last years becomes more fully available) that he was breaking new ground and deliberately departing, in important respects, from

† There has, of course, been some fruitful discussion in the Russian emigration. Most noteworthy are the brilliant essays by the late Victor Frank in *Selected Articles* (edited by Leonard Schapiro), London, 1974.

the canons of the classical Russian novel. I believe myself that – whether one thinks it for better or for worse – the latter is in fact the case, and that *Doctor Zhivago* is, within the Russian tradition of prose-writing, *sui generis* – and was consciously intended to be.

It is, perhaps, to be regretted that it is called a "novel". The word inevitably invites comparison with the great Russian novels of the past, and this has often bedevilled discussion of it. The general scope of the work, the time-span covered, and the fact that it has a narrative structure of sorts (a "story" – which could even be used to make a film in the West), has likewise led to its being judged by the same standards as such vast synoptic portraits of an age, with a large cast of elaborately drawn characters, as Tolstoi's *War and Peace*. Needless to say, anything judged by inapplicable criteria is bound to be found wanting.

Like Gladkov, Nadezhda Mandelstam was also led by the choice of the word "novel" and the superficial resemblances to Tolstoi to speak in a critical vein of *Doctor Zhivago*, judging it a failure from the point of view of what Pasternak himself said he had set out to achieve. But in the course of taking him to task, she does, it seems to me, brilliantly define what he was actually trying to do – and might more unquestionably be thought to have succeeded in, if the issue had not been confused by terminology and comparisons of dubious validity:

"I understand Pasternak better now – he was drawn [i.e. in writing *Doctor Zhivago*] by the need to 'externalize', to look at things from the outside, 'objectively'. As a poet, he was wholly dominated by his feelings, and his lyrics are essentially part and parcel of his ordinary, workaday life – this indeed is their charm. In the everyday life around him, he only rarely glimpsed 'objective' factors beyond, such as history and the country as a whole, and even then he saw them chiefly in the perspective of the immediate present. But he was prey to a nagging urge to analyse, to look at things from a distance, to see them in larger perspective. This was because he felt that for someone like himself who lived by inner feeling there was an unfortunate cleavage between subject and object. Pasternak's novel is a remembrance of things past, an attempt to determine his own place in the swift-flowing movement of days, and to seek understanding of this movement itself."

This is a perfectly true description of Pasternak's intentions, and could not be better put – though, as we have seen, his "nagging urge to analyse" was born of a sense of imperative duty, and his concern with broad historical issues and the fate of the country at large had always been greater than Mrs Mandelstam allows. The essential point is that once Pasternak had been forced by extraneous circumstances to deal with matters he would normally have thought outside the purview of a lyric poet, he had to face the difficult question: by what means was it to be done? It was a question that had exercised him long before his own experiences in later years made it almost literally a matter of life and death for him. In the immediate aftermath of the Revolution, during the twenties, he had already approached broad historical themes in long narrative poems, but he was clearly not yet very sure of his ground – as for many of his contemporaries (including Mandelstam), it was still too early for him to resolve the ambiguities in his attitude to what was going on. These poems were unfinished and, as Sinyavski says, they create the impression of long "lyrical digressions". The same is true of the various prose fragments he wrote during the twenties and thirties. Some of them anticipate *Doctor Zhivago* in general manner, themes, and occasionally in certain precise details. Already in *Without Love* (published in a newspaper in November, 1918), we find one name later used in *Doctor Zhivago* and the makings of a "plot" which would have centred on the fate of intellectuals in the Revolution. From this alone it is clear that *Doctor Zhivago* was not the caprice of a poet who late in life decided to try his hand at writing a novel, but that it was something which in form as well as in content had "matured" over many years. When, after the Terror of 1937 and its renewal in the wake of victory over the Germans, Pasternak felt in duty bound to make some extensive statement or comment on his times far beyond the scope of lyrical poetry, it was natural for him to revert to his earlier "experiments" in prose, and he certainly did so not only in full consciousness of his limitations as a novelist in the ordinary sense, but more particularly of the inadequacy of the "classical" novel as such to portray what Akhmatova called "the real, not the calendar, twentieth century", which began in Russia in 1905 and somewhat later in the West. It is possible, as Gladkov suggests, that he would have achieved his aim better by means of a more direct autobiographical account of the era (as in his much earlier *Safe Conduct*, 1931) without any of the trappings or fictional devices of the "novel". But if he considered this, he must have rejected it for several reasons. In the first place, he did not want to be tied by the literal facts of his own life. A very important and perhaps overlooked aspect of *Doctor Zhivago* is that though the central character is largely based on the author's own life,† it is at the same time a projection into the past of what this life *might*, or indeed, *should* have been, had it been more typical of what happened to Pasternak's generation: Yuri Zhivago dies of a heart attack in a suffocating Moscow street car (the "locomotive of history"?) in 1929, and this very effective image for the death of the Russian intelligentsia as a whole at the end of the twenties, in the year when Stalin achieved supremacy over his rivals, would have been impossible in a straightforward autobiographical narrative. What came later, in the thirties, for those who, like Pasternak, survived to see them, was a life in the tomb, and in *Doctor Zhivago* this is indicated by the devastatingly simple device (perhaps unprecedented of its kind in literature) of passing over those years in silence: the unspeakable cannot, by definition, be spoken of. Only in the Epilogue, set in the war-time interlude when, paradoxically, Russia again began to breathe in the midst of death, is there a backward glance at the thirties in a conversation between two friends of the poet who have survived. This too would have been impossible in an autobiography, where the author would have had to account for a whole decade in his life.

Perhaps another, more incidental reason for the choice of the "novel" form was that the very conditions under which Pasternak wrote *Doctor Zhivago* imposed a fictional disguise: he could scarcely have given the manuscript to read to other people in the Moscow of 1947-53 if the many crucial reflections on history, art and the meaning of the Revolution had been set down in his own name, instead of being presented as dialogue between invented characters living in Russia before the war, or in the twenties. Then, there is the problem of "Lara". It was Pasternak's love for Ivinskaya that sustained him throughout the period when he was at work on *Doctor Zhivago* – including the four terrible years after her arrest in 1949. Without her, and her fate, the book would probably never have been completed – it might well have petered out and remained only a fragment, like several previous attempts to write a lengthy piece of narrative prose. Yuri's relations with Lara (that is, Pasternak's with Ivinskaya) are the keystone of the work, and she personifies the whole country's betrayal, captivity and defencelessness. The

†And in some externals on that of his friend from student days, Yuri Samarin. (see note on pages 191-2)

arrest of Lara, with which the book ends, is of course a direct allusion to Ivinskaya's arrest in 1949 – though by an extraordinary kind of prophetic anticipation it was more closely paralleled in real life by her second imprisonment in 1960, a few months after Pasternak's death (the fear that the Soviet authorities would take posthumous revenge on him through her, when he was no longer there to protect her and his relative immunity no longer extended to her, haunted him constantly during his last unhappy years of persecution under the Khrushchev régime: "Tir'd with all these, from these would I be gone, Save that, to die, I leave my love alone . . ."). It would obviously have been out of the question in those years for Pasternak to describe his relations with "Lara" in other than some kind of fictional form, as a story transferred to a previous decade.

If one is to judge a work of literature by the extent to which it fulfils the author's intentions, then there is no doubt that *Doctor Zhivago* is a successful embodiment of what Pasternak set out to do – and this must *ipso facto* apply to the form as well. In his choice of means, he was of course concerned to find a way of overcoming what Mrs Mandelstam calls the "cleavage between subject and object", and he did this by the very straightforward procedure of subordinating the "objective" narrative of the conventional novel to the paramount "subjective" vision of the author; as in his lyric poetry, he remains at the centre of his universe. This may sound somewhat arbitrary, but I believe that the effect of such a characteristically "self-centred" approach was, curiously, to "legitimize" (in aesthetic terms) the use of extensive narrative prose after decades of its misapplication in the Soviet era. The main consequence of "socialist realism" when it was forcibly imposed in the thirties, was to revive and perpetuate (increasingly as an empty shell) the conventional novel as it had evolved in the nineteenth century. Ludicrous as this was, it was comprehensible as a reflection of a desire for "stability" once the revolutionary upheaval was over: it was all part of the general trend in the Stalin years to bring back some of the outward appurtenances of the old "bourgeois" society. The canon of "socialist realism" was therefore based not on the truly revolutionary prose-writers of the preceding decade (Babel, Zamiatin, and others), but on those who had already then, often consciously taking Tolstoi as their model, depicted the Revolution and its aftermath in long, panoramic novels (Sholokov, Fedin, and to some extent Leonov). In both Russia and the West, the nineteenth-century novel was the product of relatively settled, hierarchical societies, which it was possible to survey at leisure, in sometimes vastly comprehensive fashion – and often from the vantage point of a tranquil, well-to-do existence. Of the great Russian novelists, perhaps only Dostoyevski, in the "frenetic" quality of his writing, gave a foretaste of the disintegration to come – but, as Mrs Mandelstam so rightly says, it is hard to think of Dostoyevski as a mere "novelist". After the old Russian society had exploded, never to be reconstituted except (by Stalin) in a few of its most vicious and hollow aspects, it became absurd – and, what is more, an offence against "realism" – to continue writing a kind of prose appropriate only to the seemingly eternal way of life under which it had flourished. Babel understood this (in *Red Cavalry*, 1923), when he showed the Civil War much as it was seen by those who were caught up in it – as a series of brief, "cinematic" glimpses of savage and meaningless activity which went on autonomously, having no visible connection with any wider social or historical background such as a classical novelist would have supplied. The simple fact of the matter is that when a society disintegrates, it is self-evidently impossible for anyone to have an overall view of it. The tremendous, frenzied movement of people, the breakdown of normal communications and accustomed relationships, means that nobody, not even the new rulers, knows what is going on in the country or the world at large. It has been said very aptly that the individual experience of a revolutionary upheaval is like a dream: reality no longer impinges on the mind in an orderly, coherent fashion, but rather in grotesquely fragmented, apparently alogical sequences. The pattern of human contacts, normally so predictable and for the most part subject to prior co-ordination, dissolves away and life appears instead to be ruled mainly by "irrational" coincidences.

One of the chief criticisms of *Doctor Zhivago* in the West was that it relies too much on coincidences, but in this, as in other respects, Pasternak was only emphasizing the realism of his approach: anyone whose life has been catastrophically dislocated will confirm that "coincidence" plays a much larger part than in an ordinary, settled existence. During a revolution, or as a homeless refugee, you are always "running into" people at the most unlikely moments and in the most unlikely places, and such chance meetings come to seem much more natural than when they occur in the context of the stable relationships they have replaced.

Doctor Zhivago is less a novel in the usual sense than what might be called a lyrical kaleidoscope: persons, events and places pass rapidly before the reader, and there is rarely any attempt to elaborate them, let alone to place them against a general background. But that is how life was for most people during all the years of war and revolution, and throughout the subsequent Soviet era. There was no "general background", either to individual lives or to the life of the country as a whole – nobody could have the broad picture which previously, like so much else, had always been taken for granted. Other things – also once taken for granted (and not only by the privileged) – move into the foreground: the simple business of staying alive is no longer a routine, and the actual processes of daily existence assume inordinate importance. It is also part of Pasternak's "truth-to-life" that he devotes so much attention to apparently trivial matters like gathering fuel, laying in supplies of potatoes for the winter, or obtaining food by barter from a peasant woman. Such things loomed infinitely larger than "events" or the personalities supposedly in control of them: it is significant that of the three who "made" the Revolution, only Lenin is mentioned directly (and then in passing), while Stalin is referred to obliquely as a "pockmarked Caligula" in a conversation that takes place in pre-revolutionary times, and Trotski appears once under a Russified Yiddish form of his first name: "Leibochka". Another striking aspect of the disruption of reality in a revolutionary epoch is the blurring, in retrospect, of chronological distinctions. The suicide of Strelnikov in chapter 14 of *Doctor Zhivago* is something that might seem to have belonged more plausibly to the later thirties, but its "displacement" to the early twenties only enhances the sense, tellingly conveyed in *Doctor Zhivago* as a whole, that for those who, like Pasternak, survived to look back on the period from later decades, it had been like living in a trance, at some "bewitched crossroads" in history.

Doctor Zhivago, as Mrs Mandelstam says, was Pasternak's attempt to "determine his own place in the swift-flowing movement of days", and it must be judged primarily from this point of view.

Max Hayward,
Mishkenot Sha'ananim,
Jerusalem.
March 1977

ACKNOWLEDGEMENTS

I wish to express my gratitude to Janet Caldwell, who greatly eased the burden of preparing this translation for the printers, and to Valerie Jensen for her skill and perseverance in tracking down essential items of information. Tanya Litvinov and Martin Dewhirst gave generous help in reply to queries concerning persons mentioned in the text, and Dr Hayim Tadmor, of the Hebrew University, Jerusalem, providentially supplied a copy of a rare book I needed to consult.

My thanks are also due to Michael Harari for kindly granting his permission to reproduce excerpts from several of his translations of Pasternak's later poems.

M.H.

"The roofs of towns you pass,
The porch of every peasant hut,
The poplar standing at the gate
Will know you by your face"

Boris Pasternak

I

I first met Pasternak at the end of the winter in 1936, in Meyerhold's house.

Meyerhold had invited me to lunch with Pasternak and his wife, and with Malraux and his brother. The lunch went on until the evening when Malraux and his brother had to leave for the Kursk station to catch a train for the Crimea – they were going with Koltsov and Babel to see Gorki, who was ill, in Tesseli. After they had gone, I also made a move to leave, but I was asked to stay on and thus spent a long, blissful evening in the company of Pasternak, Meyerhold and their wives, drinking marvellous coffee brewed by Meyerhold himself and a brandy of rare quality. This was when the photograph was taken that still hangs over my bed: a youthful-looking Pasternak, Meyerhold and myself, young, thin and shy.

The conversation over coffee was interesting and full of significance, but it revolved entirely around Meyerhold and his situation at that time. I have given the gist of it in my book *Five Years With Meyerhold* and need not repeat it here. Unfortunately, the uniqueness of the occasion, my understandable overexcitement and the rather liberal quantities of brandy poured out by Meyerhold (which I was too shy to refuse) meant that I could not later recall everything – for which I was furious with myself the next day. All the same, however, this was the beginning of my acquaintanceship with Pasternak.

After this I quite frequently ran into him at concerts, and

he answered my greetings, but it was a long time before we had another conversation, except for one occasion when we met on Gogol Boulevard and he stopped to talk to me with quite extraordinary outspokenness. This was in the autumn of 1937, at the height of the arrests and executions. He talked while I listened, embarrassed by the unexpected vehemence of his diatribe, until he suddenly checked himself almost in mid-sentence. He was very worked up and kept referring to Dostoyevski – I remember a phrase about Shigalyov.* A little before this my brother had been arrested, and the brevity of the entry in my notebook about this meeting is eloquent enough: "Gogol Boulevard, Pasternak", and the date . . .

At the beginning of that year Pasternak had been attacked at the so-called "Pushkin plenum"* of the board of the Writers' Union – this was the price he had to pay for the praise lavished on him by Bukharin in his speech on poetry at the First Congress of Soviet Writers. Particularly harsh words were spoken by A. and X. At first sight it seems strange that X. should have made such a speech – how could X., a genuine poet of great subtlety, associate himself with this crude and demagogic assault on Pasternak? It can only be understood against the background of the psychology of those times, when fear seeped into every pore and abject cravenness became the normal standard of behaviour. Look at any newspaper from those days and you will see how tomorrow's victims, trying to save their own skins, heaped abuse on today's. In the autumn or early winter of the year before (1936), there had already been a great fuss over Pasternak's refusal to sign a protest against André Gide's *Retour de l'URSS*.* Pasternak had excused himself by saying he had not read the book – which was the literal truth, but neither had nine tenths of all those writers who agreed to sign. Pasternak's moral squeamishness struck the others as affected and provocative though nothing could have been

* Asterisks refer to notes at the back.

34

further from what he intended. I remember a writer called V. who had signed and was quite genuinely indignant with Pasternak: "Well, he didn't read it, but so what? Neither did I. Does he think any of the others did? Why does he want to be different from everybody else? The book was denounced as lies in *Pravda*, wasn't it? . . ." This episode was the beginning of Pasternak's conflict with the Writers' Union which came to a head so dramatically during the days when he was awarded the Nobel Prize – then, too, most of the writers who condemned him had not read his book.

For a long time afterwards he was not published. It was not until just before the war that a small volume of his translations came out and *Young Guard* printed his version of *Hamlet*.

In the spring of 1940 he gave a reading of his *Hamlet* in the Moscow University Club on Herzen Street. The meeting was open to the public and had been advertised beforehand. Vsevolod Loboda, a young poet (who was killed early in the War), and I bought tickets for it. After his rather long silence, it was good to hear Pasternak reading again in his organ-like, nasal voice, accentuating words in his own unexpected manner. He looked young and in good spirits. I was even more pleased, however, by the enthusiastic, sensitive and sophisticated reaction of the audience in the crowded hall. It consisted for the most part of students from Moscow University and MIFLI,* that miraculous generation just at the beginning of the forties which included Pavel Kogan, Kulchitski, Mayorov, Gudzenko and Slutski.

I remember coming home and writing something in my diary about my delight at this marvellous audience – not, of course, foreseeing the fate in store for a generation which was soon to be all but wiped out in two wars.*

Loboda, who was longing to meet Pasternak, persuaded me to go and look for him backstage. I found him standing in the middle of a large room, surrounded by young women to whom he was holding forth in a loud voice and with great verve about Goethe, Herder and Shakespeare, while they looked at him with smiles on their faces – when Pasternak became excited about something it was impossible not to smile at the utterly pure and natural way in which he assumed that everyone else must be just as interested as he. He did not notice Loboda and me, and we dared not interrupt him. When we went out on the street, the first thunderstorm of summer had just ended. There were still rumblings in the distance, and the air was full of ozone, the fragrance of young May lime blossom, and the organ music of Pasternak's verse.

That evening somehow reminded me of another evening at the beginning of the thirties when I had first seen Pasternak and heard him read. It was in the FOSP Club* – that same "Rostov" mansion which still houses the Union of Soviet Writers – in a small, inconvenient hall with double rows of windows, a low stage and a tiny room behind it. It was the same hall in which the dead Mayakovski had lain in state in April 1930. Pasternak read *Spektorski*,* which he had only just completed. He came out on the stage, very young and handsome, smiled in a diffident, friendly way, showing his white teeth, and began to make some quite unneeded explanatory remarks, rambling on until he suddenly stopped in embarrassment, said "Well, you'll see for yourselves", or words to that effect, smiled again and began to recite in his drawling manner: "Accustomed to picking out the raisins of various harmonies from the sweet bun of life . . ."* Even now, over thirty years later, I can still reproduce his every intonation and as I write this, his deep, low voice, with its nasal timbre, still sounds in my ears: "Space sleeps, in love with space . . .",* while the fragrance of the lime trees drifted in through the open windows, together with the noise of the No. 26 tram clanging down Herzen Street.

I had fallen in love with Pasternak's verse a few years before, when I was still a schoolboy. The first of his books to come into my hands was the little white volume with his portrait on the cover, put out in the *Ogoniok** series. Here I came across the group of poems entitled *The Rift,** and with a youthful passion for anything dramatic, began to declaim them to myself under my breath even before I knew whether I really liked them or not. Mayakovski, about whom I had long been very enthusiastic, never missing a single appearance by him, had quoted a stanza from "Marburg"* in "How to Make Verse" and described it as brilliant. This was quite enough for me to learn the whole of "Marburg" off by heart. Love was not preceded by understanding – it was rather the other way round. Very soon everything published by Pasternak had become part of the equipment of my young mind. Every summer shower began to seem like a quotation from him, as did every misty dawn, every garden splashed with morning dew – thanks to the magic of his poetry the whole natural landscape of the townsman now lost its tedious look of everyday familiarity and became once again a shining, vibrant miracle; a lilac bush in the backyard was no longer to be outdone by a romantic oak on a crag, or Yesenin's birch trees. Pasternak's neo-romanticism did not summon the reader to exotic places, to faraway seas and mountains, but was perfectly at home with a bench on Gogol Boulevard, a bathing-hut on the Klyazma* or in Neskuchny Sad.* He took all the familiar things he had known from childhood and turned them into poetry: the town and its streets, husks of sunflower seeds, the taste of a piece of orange, a garden gleaming under the rain at night, the languor of a waltz, bookshelves with tomes by ancient philosophers and historians. He combined in some marvellous way the immortal, almost meaningless warblings of Fet's nightingale with the irony of Heine, the philosophical flights of Tiutchev with the sensuous music of the impressionists. The truly poetic is always closer to the "non-poetic" than to the clichés of popular ballad-mongers who convert the golden sovereigns of Pushkin and Lermontov into a coinage of common brass. The generation which early took a fancy to Pasternak immediately crossed a frontier

37

in matters of poetic taste from which there was no turning back: "a lilac branch / rainsodden like a sparrow";* "raindrops weighty as cufflinks";* "an evening empty as an interrupted tale, / left unfinished by a star".* The inner world of the young is complex, and this kind of yearning for simplicity is only acceptable to them if it is genuine and unaffected. For me and my contemporaries there was no feeling that Pasternak's poetry was incompatible with Mayakovski's – on the contrary, it was complementary to it, adding depth and perspective. Of his living contemporaries Mayakovski described only two as geniuses: Khlebnikov and Pasternak. In those days, incidentally, there was no question at all of setting off the one against the other as opposites, and nobody ever tried to force on us the false dilemma of having to choose between them.

In later years reading or re-reading Pasternak could affect me in many different ways, and here I am speaking only of how he struck me on first acquaintance, when he first entered my life as a poet. There were many more encounters in later life when his volumes of poetry always opened at pages needed at some particular moment and when the re-reading of familiar lines provided the key which enabled me to get the measure of whatever at the time happened to be confusing my mind or spirits, thus helping me to come out of it unscathed.

In the summer of 1933 his *Second Birth** was published. All I now remember from that summer are the constant rain showers, this slender volume with the stylized drawing of a piano on the cover, and also who was reading it and in what place. No deliberate effort was required to memorize the poems in it – once you had read them, they simply stayed in the mind. They were poems in the true sense: brief and remarkably precise, impossible to paraphrase. Like those of *My Sister Life** and *Above the Barriers,** you immediately adopted them as formulations of spiritual experience, as a shorthand transcript of feelings which enabled you to conjecture in a flash of illumination what it was like to go through many things still only in store for you.

A little earlier, at first in extracts in *Zvezda,** *Safe Conduct** had appeared and had also become one of those books you take with you in your suitcase, wherever you may be going, because you hate to be without it and can always open it at random, at any page, and find something new. No sooner had it come out than it was promptly denounced for "idealism" and the label has stuck to this very day. Some passages I still find difficult, but I am sure this is my fault, not the author's. The chapters on his childhood, on the beginnings of his poetry, on his first love, on Scriabin, Rilke and Mayakovski I regard as equal to the very best in Russian prose.

In subsequent years Pasternak occasionally re-appeared in the pages of the literary journals, only to disappear again for long periods after being anathematized by the critics. He had a talent for getting into ambiguous political situations not of his own making – as when he was praised by Bukharin, or became drawn into the affair of Gide's book.

I heard Pasternak's speech at the First Congress of Soviet Writers. This was at the end of the summer of 1934. In December of the same year the decade was rent asunder by the bullet fired at Kirov. The assassination of Kirov signalled the beginning of Stalin's purges of his enemies, real and imagined. Everybody thought the mass expulsions from Leningrad were a local and isolated measure – only the future was to show that they were a prelude to the terror of 1937 and later years.

Until the end of 1936 the state of affairs in literature had not noticeably worsened, and even the arrest of Osip Mandelstam in May 1934 had not caused any particular alarm. It was only after the death of Gorki in the summer of 1936 that events started to get out of hand. Pasternak was by then spending a lot of his time translating the Georgian poets.* A one-volume edition of his own work came out in two editions, though in the second the lines in the poem

39

"A High Illness"* at the end of the passage describing Lenin's speech to the Ninth Congress of Soviets were cut: "A genius comes as a harbinger of betterment, / and his going is avenged with tyranny." They showed the unpolitical poet to be a better prophet than all our seasoned men of the world.

I have a very precise memory, from the beginning of the thirties, of the times during which Pasternak was "accepted" and those during which he was ostracized. He was accepted right till the end of 1936, that is, up to the trouble over Gide's book. The high points in this period were Stalin's telephone call to him after Mandelstam's arrest* and the ovation he received at the end of his speech to the Writers' Congress. He was later "in disgrace" for almost four years, until about the middle of 1940, when the attitude towards him softened perceptibly, during the brief interlude of general relaxation no doubt dictated by the looming danger of war. A volume of his translations appeared and his *Hamlet*, completed in those years, was also published. It was at this time that Anna Akhmatova was able to publish a new collection of her verse, *From Six Books*, which included her poem on Pasternak with its last line: "And the whole of the earth was his to inherit, and his to share with every human spirit." This period of relative tolerance lasted into the first post-war years, until March 1947, when the newspaper *Culture and Life** published a savage attack on Pasternak, opening a new period of "disgrace" which was to end only with Stalin's death. Apart from translations, no work by him appeared in print again until 1954, when *Znamia** published a cycle of poems from *Doctor Zhivago*. I read these while I was still in the camp. By the time I returned to Moscow the manuscript of the novel itself was already being passed from hand to hand. Everybody expected it to appear both in *Znamia* and as a book – even the name of the man who would do the editing was mentioned and nobody imagined that it would soon become forbidden fruit. A large new collection of Pasternak's verse was also being prepared for publication.* But in 1957 the novel came out in Italy, and

40

in the following year Pasternak was awarded the Nobel Prize. In the late autumn of 1958 he was expelled from the Union of Soviet Writers. It was at the height of these events that I saw him for the last time. Our most frequent meetings were during and immediately after the war, when he had already finished *Hamlet* and was coming to the end of *Romeo and Juliet*. These were also the years in which he worked on *Antony and Cleopatra* and wrote new verse of his own: *On Early Trains*,* the poem on Marina Tsvetayeva's death,* *Earth's Space** and the *Zhivago* cycle. He was also writing the novel itself. He started and then abandoned a long poem about everyday life during the war.

During this whole period I kept more or less detailed notes of my conversations with him – mostly, of course, of what was said by him. Despite all my subsequent troubles, I was able to preserve these notes, which now form the basic core of this memoir. Everything else is simply intended to provide background – the circumstances of time and place – to the record of our conversations.

At the very end of autumn, 1941, I found myself in Chistopol,* together with other members of the Writers' Union who had been evacuated there. By the time I arrived Pasternak had been there a few weeks already. Tsvetayeva was no longer there – she had been more or less forced by trouble over her residence permit to move further up the Kama, to Yelabuga, where her life was to end.

Chistopol, a small, run-of-the-mill provincial town, took on a strange appearance with the arrival of evacuees from Moscow and Leningrad. An odd touch was added by the writers, of whom there must have been several dozen. In their stylish overcoats and soft felt hats they wandered through the streets – which were covered with good Russian mud – as though they were still in the corridors of their building on Vorovski Street. It was impossible not to run into them several times a day. They all drew their money through a branch of V.U.O.A.P.* set up in the second storey of a wooden house; they all ate in a tiny restaurant opposite the building of the District Party Committee; they all went to read the Moscow newspapers in the Party reading-room and borrowed books from the local Teachers' Club.†

The writers' colony on the banks of the Kama did not last very long in this form. Already in the first months of 1942 it began to break up, as its younger and more enterprising members started to leave. Arbuzov and I left in the middle of March, a little after Pavel Shubin, Vs. Bagritski and others.

Pasternak returned to Moscow at the end of 1942, but went back to spend the winter in Chistopol. He again returned to Moscow for the summer of 1943 – at first he was by himself, but later he brought his family as well.

My first conversation with him in Chistopol consisted mostly of reminiscences about our previous meetings. It was still less than two years since Meyerhold had perished and for a long time nobody knew any details – he had simply vanished, like so many others in those days. There was a host of rumours about his end, all totally untrue, as later appeared. We began by talking about these stories – which in itself set a tone of frankness and mutual trust during this first exchange.

Pasternak's existence in Chistopol in the winter of 1941–2 was far from being a "sweet bun of life". Materially, he lived worse than most other writers, particularly the "giants" of literature – some of these rented whole houses, but Pasternak had to make do with one small uncomfortable room on Volodarski Street. The contrast between his living conditions and those of Leonov or Fedin, for example, was

† Among them at that time were: L. Leonov, K. Fedin, N. Aseyev, K. Trenev, V. Shklovski, M. Isakovski, D. Petrovski, A. Derman, G. Munblit, S. Gekht, A. Glebov, A. Yavich, G. Vinokur, N. Gudzi, P. Shubin, S. Galkin, P. Arski, M. Zenkevich, V. Bokov, A. Erlikh, A. Pismenny, Hugo Huppert, M. Ruderman, S. Levman, A. Arbuzov, A. Leites, V. Parnakh, M. Petrovykh, M. Dobrynin, Vs. Bagritski, I. Nusinov and others. There were also a great many writers' wives. Among those who came to visit their families were: A. Fadeyev, A. Surkov, S. Lipkin, M. Lifshits and E. Dolmatovski.

quite striking. Leonov even kept a special watchman to stand guard with a shotgun over his suitcases at night; he also bought honey by the barrel at the otherwise poorly-stocked local market, where the prices soon rose sky-high. Another man of letters, in order to make himself independent of the meat supplies in the market, bought a whole bull for himself. But the majority of the writers lived in great straits. I remember how G., the story writer, was reduced to selling his wife's underwear in the market, for which, of course, he got very little because of his inexperience. (At the same market, G.'s brother-in-law, the poet A., who had brought his large savings with him and lived very well, wandered round with a sack buying up various objects at bargain prices.) Valentin Parnakh, the poet and translator who had once made his living in Paris as a musician and dancer, whose book of verse had been illustrated by Picasso and who now looked like a large parrot in his battered foreign hat, received two bowls of soup in the restaurant for minding the door and seeing that people closed it properly. The place was not heated, and the temperature was the same as outside in the street. People always kept their outer clothing on – except Pasternak who unfailingly took off his coat and hat, hanging them on a nail on the wall. What is more, he always brought his work with him: an English-Russian dictionary, a pocket edition of Shakespeare and whatever page he had just done of his translation. I also remember the long slips of paper on which he wrote out difficult passages. He worked while waiting for his portion of thin cabbage soup (even this was soon to run out).

One of the hardest problems of life in Chistopol was firewood. Householders would only rent rooms to lodgers who could supply their own. At one point the local Soviet allotted the writers several cubic metres of frozen firewood which was stacked a long way off on the bank of the Kama. For some reason there was no proper access to it, and it first had to be manhandled over the road. The well-to-do minority hired people to fetch it for them, but most of us had to go and carry it ourselves. I worked side by side with Pasternak. He did not complain, but got down to hauling the logs, if not with pleasure, at least cheerfully and with a will – yet there were almost thirty degrees of frost that day.

Because of the absurd way in which the stoves were situated it was always cold in the room rented by Pasternak and his wife. He complained that his fingers often went numb while he was writing. You could only get to it by walking through a kitchen used by everybody else in the house – there were always three Primus stoves going there at full blast. Sometimes, to let in a little warmth, Pasternak kept the door to the kitchen open. The noise of the Primuses was often accompanied by the sound of a gramophone playing Utesov, the Piatnitski choir, or some popular tango or other. All this carried over into the room where Pasternak worked. His wife, Zinaida Nikolayevna, was out most of the time: she taught in a boarding school for orphans maintained by the Union of Writers where she was provided with two meals a day. She brought the evening meal home and shared it with him. Even in these conditions Pasternak did not lose heart: "I am alone from morning to night", he said cheerfully, when I came to see him the first time, "but at least I can work without interruption." He tried to see something good in all these inconveniences and hardships: "At least we are closer to the basic things of life here," he often said. "Everybody should live like this during the war, particularly writers . . ."

I have rarely met anyone so patient, so unspoilt, and with such a capacity to endure as Pasternak. Simplicity and a modest way of life seemed to be part of his nature. His neighbour at Peredelkino,* the playwright Afinogenov, has a note in his diary (Autumn, 1937) in which he marvels at Pasternak's undemanding and simple character, and says that someone of his temperament would get on easily anywhere – even in a prison cell. Just at that time Afinogenov was anxiously expecting to be arrested any moment, and he was able to share his fears with Pasternak, who also, of course, was by no means immune to the same danger. To be sent to a forced labour camp was not easy for anyone, but it was hardest of all on people attached to a comfortable existence, and the good things of life. When I was in a camp myself I often thought of Pasternak and felt that even there he would have been just as serene, cheerful and amiable. I am not suggesting that evacuation is comparable to life in a camp, but I believe that for some people imprisonment might have been easier. If Tsvetayeva had gone to a camp instead of to Yelabuga, I believe she might have survived – at least she would have been more likely to find moral support, human warmth, friendship and medical help.

Once, when the gramophone in the kitchen had been blaring away for several hours on end, Pasternak could stand it no longer and ran out to plead with his hosts, asking them in hesitant, rather rambling phrases to let him get on with his work. I gathered this only from Pasternak's own account of the incident. Apparently the people in the kitchen did stop the gramophone, muttering something about "all this fuss". But Pasternak could do no more work that day. He paced the room, cursing himself for his lack of self-control and patience, for being so fastidious and over-weening, for being so unpardonably arrogant as to put the interests of his own work – no use, perhaps, to anyone at all – above the need for recreation of these people who could scarcely be blamed if they had never been taught to appreciate good music, and so on and so forth. That same evening there was a public meeting in honour of the Red Army, at which the evacuated writers read their work. When it was Pasternak's turn he came out on the stage, but suddenly refused to read, saying that he had no right after what had happened that morning, and thought it his duty to offer a public apology to the people concerned, etc. etc. The representatives of the town authorities were quite taken aback and frowned unhappily; the writers tittered, and the audience in the crowded hall looked baffled. I remember the embarrassed expression on Fedin's face. Losing the

45

thread of what he was saying, Pasternak suddenly got stuck in the middle of a word and, in despair at having confused and complicated matters even further, left the meeting. I went out after him, and for a long time we wandered among the snow-drifts. I had enough sense not to make any comment on what had happened and mentioned instead the rumours about the fantastic new victories of our armies, the taking of Briansk, Kharkov, Poltava, Kiev and Odessa, and speculated on the reasons why no official announcement had yet been made.

Pasternak quite often provoked smiles or laughter by some display of gaucherie. During the First Congress of Soviet Writers a group of workers building the Moscow Metro came to offer their greetings. Among them were some girls in the rubber suits which they wore on the job. One of them was carrying a heavy metal tool on her shoulder, and it so happened that she took up her position next to Pasternak who was sitting on the platform waiting for his turn to speak. He immediately jumped up and tried to take the tool away from her, but the girl would not give it up. Pasternak had not realized that it was part of an intended theatrical effect and had simply wanted to relieve her of the burden. Watching this tussle between them, the audience burst into laughter. Pasternak was covered with confusion and began his speech by trying to explain what had happened.

The high comedy of the incident lay in the fact that the heavy tool on the girl's shoulder was there not out of necessity but for the sake of a ritual both contrived and false, which was supposed to symbolize her function as a worker; with his direct and natural view of things, Pasternak failed to perceive this and saw only a frail woman struggling with an unwieldy metal object. When the audience began to laugh, he himself soon smiled in embarrassment at his blunder – though if anybody deserved to be laughed at, it was the organizers of this pseudo-theatrical stunt.

It was a peculiar feature of the age that everybody had

grown completely accustomed to such ostentation and bogus expressions of public sentiment; nobody was surprised at the sight of a woman unnecessarily shouldering a pickaxe – any more than by the vast rhymed tributes from the entire nation to the Great Leader, or by the long columns of birthday greetings to him printed in the newspapers for many months on end after the event. All this is still not very long ago, but it already seems strange to the point of being almost incredible; yet at the time it seemed strange if somebody was so eccentric as not to take these ritual obeisances seriously.

It is not true, as one young memoirist has written, that such "strange" behaviour was deliberately "put on" by Pasternak. This may have been the impression of people who had quite forgotten what it was to behave naturally on any occasion – something that of course looked "comic" to all those who lived by pretence and social convention. Diplomats and trimmers always regard straightforward and honest behaviour as naivety bordering on folly. There were a good many such "follies" in Pasternak's life, but they were of the kind about which Anatole France once said "they are only rarely committed by fools, and much more often by the very wise."

When in the summer of 1934 Stalin suddenly phoned Pasternak and asked him what he thought of Mandelstam (who had just been arrested), the conversation ended abruptly with Stalin hanging up on him in mid-sentence, and for a long time afterwards Pasternak was in despair, reproaching himself for not having found words of sufficient weight to help Mandelstam in his plight, and for having angered the Great Leader by a familiarity of tone out of keeping with the occasion. According to Mandelstam's widow, Nadezhda Yakovlevna, "Pasternak talked with Stalin in the same way as he talked with anyone else – with me, with Anna Andreyevna [Akhmatova], with no matter who. For this very reason, his point was made beautifully – in a quite unexpected way, really hitting the nail on the

47

head. All three of us – A.A., O.E. [Mandelstam] and myself were very impressed." (Quoted from a letter from Nadezhda Mandelstam.) From a severely practical point of view, however, Pasternak's handling of the conversation was the height of naivety – it did little good to Mandelstam and queered his own pitch with Stalin – but even at this level he remained true to himself, the most natural of men.

The following chapter consists of the diary I kept in Chistopol, or rather those entries from it that refer to Pasternak, my meetings and conversations with him. They were made immediately after the occasions concerned, in small, black, cloth-bound exercise books with squared paper. I give them here almost without cuts.

2

Chistopol. November 1941

The *Litfund** dining-room is on the corner of Tolstoi and Volodarski Streets. You enter directly from the street, and there is no lobby. The door opens and shuts all the time, people come in and out, sit down, or stand about, earnestly discussing the news from the front, or wondering if it is going to be a hard winter and whether to move to Tashkent while the going is good, before the Kama has completely frozen over; or how to get firewood, or a permit for a brighter lightbulb from the City Soviet. The only one to sit here all by himself, talking with no one, from the morning until the hour when the dining-room closes, is Valentin Parnakh, a small man with an unhappy, almost frozen face; the collar of his once stylish coat, now much the worse for wear, is turned up and he is still wearing his brown Parisian hat. Then there is the rawboned Dmitri Petrovski in a leather jacket and red scarf, his face scored by harsh wrinkles, and with grey, almost matted hair and wild eyes, constantly on the move – coming in, or going out, only to return the next moment; Victor Borisovich Shklovski, spry, portly, ironical and curious, but slightly unsure of himself, always taking a very close look at everything, chatting with all and sundry, but thinking his own private thoughts; Leonid Leonov, who has grown a moustache and begun to look like a foreigner; Glebov, calm, cheerful and eternally busy; Aseyev, small and like a pike; Fedin, trying to play the part of a country gentleman and putting on airs with his pipe –

but it all strikes a false note, and lacks conviction; Pismenny, full of sound, very prosaic common sense; Gekht, nervous and very restless; Mikhail Ruderman, sunk in gloom and boredom, with his nose constantly running; Munblit, with a hoarse cough and greenish complexion, like a large bird; Erlikh, pale and courteous; Hugo Huppert, always surprised at everything; G. Vinokur, clever and taciturn; S. Galkin, very good-looking; Pavel Arski, veteran contributor to *Pravda*, as rugged as an oak; Trenev, always scowling and unfriendly. And many others. Among them, standing out in cheerful contrast, is Boris Leonidovich Pasternak – graceful, benevolent, trusting, absorbed in himself and his work.

November 15
Pasternak stopped me today on the square by the District Party Committee. I had already run into him several times and exchanged greetings with him – but, as it now turned out, he had not been able to think where and when we had met before:

"I say, your face is extremely familiar . . ."

"Yes, we have met before, Boris Leonidovich."

"But where, where?"

I reminded him of our lunch with Meyerhold.

"Yes, yes, now I remember . . . of course, yes, yes, I remember very well indeed . . ."

We talked briefly about Meyerhold, and his face clouded over. Then he asked me how I came to be in Chistopol, etc.

He was in a black fur coat and black Astrakhan hat. The grey in his hair is already noticeable, but only slightly. He still looks pretty young for his age.

I walked along Volodarski Street with him. He lives right at the end of it, opposite the town park. Today was a glorious Russian winter day.

None of the other writers here has anything but harsh words for Chistopol, but Pasternak says he likes it. He invited me to his room, but I was in a hurry to get home, so we arranged to meet the following week. He seems in good spirits, and not at all thrown off his balance like most of the others. He tells me that Shklovski left yesterday for Alma-Ata.* The Kama is not yet completely frozen, but the boats are no longer running – we have had no mail for four days.

December 1

The first meeting of the poetry section [of the Writers' Union] in the Teachers' Club. As the author of a play in verse I was invited, though I have still not been formally elected to the Writers' Union.

Three hours of empty talk about nothing. Pasternak wasn't there. Present were: Aseyev, Zenkevich, Obradovich, Kolychev, Ruderman, Petrovski, Shubin, Bokov, Huppert, Arski, Bugayevski, and a few others. In a way I was the hero of the day. A week ago we received *Izvestia* of November 16 with a report headed "In the Leningrad Theatres" and saying that my play *Sons of Glory** has had a great success in the Comedy Theatre. Everybody here is like a fish out of water, cut off from their publishers and editors, feeling unwanted and forgotten, and the fact that someone in Chistopol has had a première somewhere is big news. When I ran into him the other day, Pasternak also congratulated me. He was very friendly, and every time we have one of these brief, casual meetings, I curse myself for not having kept the conversation going longer.

December 10

Went to the dining-room. It was cold, but Pasternak had taken off his coat and put it on the chair next to him. Seeing me, he invited me to join him at his table, but warned me apologetically that he would be getting on with his work even while he ate. To the right of his bowl of thin, cold cabbage soup he had four small sheets of paper. Between spoonfuls of soup he looked through them, making corrections. With his thoughts first and foremost on his work, he seems utterly out of place among the others, who sit there glumly in their fur coats, doing nothing.

December 17
Today Fedin read from his reminiscences of Gorki in the Teachers' Club. Before it began, Pasternak was very agitated, trying to make his wife comfortable – for some reason she looked peeved. First he put her next to the stove, and then moved her further away, in case it got too hot. He was astonishingly attentive and openly showed his tenderness. The small room was crammed with the local élite. Fedin, as lordly as ever, came a little late, no doubt by design, carrying a smart-looking folder. Out of it he took his manuscript, neatly typed on excellent paper and threaded together with a red tape. He asked for water to be brought – the first to jump up to go and fetch it was Pasternak, but someone got in ahead of him. When the carafe and glass appeared, Fedin carefully placed everything in front of him to form a symmetrical pattern and began to read in a slow, very theatrical manner, imitating Gorki's broad pronunciation of the letter "o" in the dialogue passages. It was certainly well done, but all a little too pat somehow. He played up the funny bits for all he was worth, and started to laugh before anyone else. Pasternak kept looking round, as though inviting us all to share his own delight. He is a remarkably good listener, always ready to laugh and show his appreciation. I talked with him in the intermission. He was quite elated. There is something old-fashioned about his generosity, something chivalrous, and not in the least bit obsequious. He is not at all concerned to stand on his own dignity in a way so typical of all the others. Compared with him even my friend Arbuzov seems much more solemn and prim.

I watched him as he listened. Most of the others were reserved and self-importantly polite. Nobody else had Pasternak's boyish expression of delight. Perhaps he looks so young because of his missing front tooth. He smiled all the time, and occasionally murmured to himself. Fedin's ugly daughter Nina gazed reverentially at her papa. Khesin, our financial overlord, sat sprawling on a divan, and listened with a condescending, supercilious air. Ruderman could hardly wait for the intermission – he kept taking out his tobacco pouch and then putting it back again. Trenev was glum and had his mind on other things. Derman had a sly smile, as though he had caught the author out in something. Erlikh looked utterly impassive. Gekht blinked and screwed up his eyes. At rare but regular intervals Fedin took a sip of water from the glass in front of him. It was all very seemly, staid and literary.

In the intermission Pasternak asked me to let him have my play to read. I said I would, though I am not sure whether I will. I am worried that he may have asked me out of his usual kindness. And then, it is hard for me to imagine Pasternak reading my verse.

December 18

I again sat with Pasternak at lunch in the *Litfund* dining-room. There was very thin soup with rice and an almost inedible stew made of something politely described as mutton. Pasternak chewed zestfully on a crust of black bread. We talked about the latest military and political developments. I told him about the vandalism of the Germans in Yasnaya Polyana* (which I heard this morning on the radio), and he was shocked, bewildered, almost incredulous.

December 20

A very cold day. Our forces have taken Ruza, Tarusa and Khalino. This was announced on the news this morning. While our armchair strategists (Leonov, Leites, Levman, Derman, Munblit, Huppert and others) were in the V.U.O.A.P. office discussing these events and jointly planning the next offensives as they puffed away at their *makhorka** cigarettes, Pasternak came in, cheerful and rosy-cheeked from the bitter cold; after greeting everybody, he went through to Khesin, reminding me as he passed by that

I had promised him my play. We made a date for the day after tomorrow.

December 22

I went to see Pasternak this afternoon. He lives in a small room which has to be entered through a filthy kitchen where there seems to be a constant din. On his table he has dictionaries, a small volume of Shakespeare, and Victor Hugo's book on Shakespeare in the original French. When I picked this up, Pasternak said how good it was, and what a pity I wasn't able to read it. I have only one copy of my play here – a version prepared by the Distribution Department, with all the many typing errors corrected by me in ink that has blotched on the atrocious paper, but Pasternak did not mind at all. He asked only whether he could take his time over reading it, since "I hate reading things all at one go".

On my way home I looked in at V.U.O.A.P. where Khesin told me he would be receiving a call that evening from G. G. Shtain, an adviser to the Arts Committee, who had asked him to get me, Pasternak and Glebov to the phone. I said I would pass this on to Pasternak and went back to him. I entered the room terrified that he might already have read the first few pages of my play and would now hand it straight back to me, but – oh bliss! – it was still lying where I had put it, and he was sitting and working.

I met him again this evening at the Regional Party Committee, where we were supposed to take Shtain's call. Apart from Glebov and Pasternak, Petrovski came along too. We waited two hours for the call. Pasternak, Glebov and I spent the time chatting, but Petrovski just sat there glowering. I was the first to be called to the phone, to be given the welcome news that my play had been accepted for publication, and that the Theatre of the Revolution would, after all, be putting it on in Tashkent. I told Shtain about the new play I was doing with Arbuzov.* Pasternak asked me to wait while he talked with Shtain – there was some question about payment for his translations, and he complained that he was very hard up. After this conversation he became nervous and almost dejected – something very unlike him. I walked along with him and soon we were sitting in his room again. Zinaida Nikolayevna was on duty at the *Litfund* orphanage. He told me that he finished *Romeo and Juliet* the other day, but is himself very dissatisfied with it. He said he regretted the war had upset all the plans to put on his translation of *Hamlet*, which he liked best of all. I was going on from him to a concert at the Teachers' Club by the woman pianist Loiter. He was in no mood to be alone and went with me.

At the concert, in a small hall lit by a paraffin lamp, everybody sat in fur coats and hats. Pasternak tried to take his coat off and I almost had to use force to stop him – the cold was quite infernal. Loiter played Bach, Beethoven, Liszt and Tchaikovsky. Pasternak is a remarkable listener. He applauded with everybody else and then went behind the scenes to kiss the hand of the pianist, a small plain Jewish woman with round glasses who was wearing three woollen jumpers. I saw P. home. The whole day was spent with him.

December 25
I met P. at lunch in the dining-room. He asked me to sit at his table. We had watery cabbage soup, and the 222 grammes of black bread issued with it. There was nothing to follow. After lunch he invited me for a walk. It was less cold today. We went past the cathedral down to the Kama and turned right to the creek.

We talked about many things. First of all about his *Hamlet*. He is depressed at the failure to get it on the stage. He rates it very high – perhaps too high – compared with everything else he has done, even his original work. He complained that the more serious a translation, the less chance there is of it providing any income: "Believe me, Shakespeare brings in nothing, but the Georgian poets provided me with enough to live on for a year or eighteen months . . ." Next we talked about what might happen once the war was over. He spoke of Stalin as a new Skalozub,* who will line us all up in military formation and order us about even more harshly: "If things remain the same after the War as they were before, I may well land up somewhere in the Far North among many of my old friends, because I shan't be able to go on not being myself . . ."

He has read the first two acts of *Long, Long Ago*, and says they are amusing, lively and elegant, but perhaps with "a little too much packed into them" – "Haven't you rather overdone the background and the period flavour?" But he added at once that this was only a very preliminary comment, and that we will have a proper talk as soon as he has read all four acts.

He questioned me about my further plans. He was very taken by my idea of writing a heroic drama based on the life of Petöfi. He has recently translated some of his verse, and read his biography with interest. He talked intriguingly about the "wild Gypsy spirit" of his poetry. He advised me to read Franz Liszt's study of the Gypsy element in Hungarian music and to familiarize myself with Lenau (I confessed I have only a very poor knowledge of him). If I can get hold of a volume of Lenau in German here, he will be glad to read him out in translation for me . . . Next we got on to Marina Tsvetayeva. When I spoke very enthusiastically about her play, *The End of Casanova*, he said he was sorry not to have read it, or to have "inexcusably forgotten it". We talked about her death in Yelabuga, "somewhere over there, look" – he pointed in the general direction further up the Kama. Then we talked again about his *Romeo and Juliet*, about translation as an art, about Lunacharski's translations, which are better than might be expected (particularly his versions of Petöfi), and then about *Hamlet* again. Once more he said how sorry he is that the Arts Theatre has decided not to put it on, and he told an anecdote about Livanov in the

Kremlin. We also talked about many other things . . . :

"A genius is nothing more than an exceptional and outstanding representative of the ordinary, average run of humanity in his own age, its immortal embodiment. A genius is closer to the ordinary man, is more akin to him than to the sort of people who congregate round the Bohemian fringes of the literary world. A genius is a quantitative extension of a mankind which is homogeneous in quality. The distance separating a genius from an ordinary man is imaginary, or rather non-existent, but this supposedly intervening space is crowded with all those 'fascinating' people who make a point of letting their hair grow long and wearing velvet jackets. It is these – if one grants that they have any place at all in history – who embody the concept of mediocrity. If a genius stands in contrast to anyone, it is not to the general public, but to the kind of set which so often, without waiting to be invited, forms a coterie around him. There is no ordinary man who is not potentially a genius."

"You will probably be surprised to hear that I prefer Demyan Bedny to the majority of Soviet poets. It is not only that he is a historical figure from the Revolution in its most dramatic stages – the Civil War and War Communism – but for me he is the Hans Sachs of our popular uprising. He is completely immersed in the naturalness of his vocation – something that cannot be said of Mayakovski, for example, who used all this as the fulcrum for only part of his energies. You have to look at figures such as Demyan Bedny not from the standpoint of poetic technique, but from that of history. I am quite unconcerned about the various individual features of any form as a whole – as long as it is primary and authentic, as long as there is no intrusion of derivative elements, of striving after false effects, of bad taste, the taste of the mediocre as I understand it. It is a matter of complete indifference to me *what* fuels the passion

57

which leads a man to play a major part in life, as long as he does play such a part . . ."

"Apropos of Mayakovski's phrase – which is true on the whole but has not been properly understood – I should say that we do not need several Mayakovskis or several Demyan Bednys. Every poet is by his very nature unique, and his value lies only in this fact of his uniqueness and authenticity. Aseyev, who was a real poet, sacrificed his gift out of loyalty to Mayakovski. But this sacrifice – as perhaps is always the case – was uncalled for . . . To achieve maturity, Pushkin needed Delvig, Tumanski, Kozlov and Bogdanovich, but we need only Pushkin and Baratynski. Poetry is a collective phenomenon in the sense that its boundlessly ramified individuality takes possession of many poets, but these many poets are needed only until one such as Pushkin appears."

"I have often marvelled at the ease with which people distinguish good lines of verse from bad ones, as though it were a question of standard parts made to fit some machine or other. What is generally referred to as bad verse is simply not verse at all. I often feel indeed that there is no such thing as good or bad verse, but that there are only good and bad poets – in other words, that any particular line exists only as part of a mental system which may be either creative or sterile. The same line may be considered good or bad according to which kind of poetic system it occurs in . . ."

"A poet must have the courage, when he changes the range of his themes and subject matter, to be prepared to write badly for a while – or to appear to do so. Not of course badly in an absolute sense, but only by his own previous standards. This is how I wrote after *Second Birth*. I did it quite consciously – otherwise I could never have dealt with a field involving public affairs,* where everything has to be tricked out in generalities, with little scope for imagery or concrete detail . . ."

"The first mark of talent is boldness. Not boldness on the stage or in an editorial office, but boldness in the presence of a blank sheet of paper . . ."

"Bad taste is always much worse than downright lack of it . . ."

"What appeals to me nowadays in poetry is precision, strength and the sort of inner restraint that clothes all personal, still warm and smouldering things – all real and uninvented private particulars – in a general, universally accessible form of expression. I dream of a style which I would call unobtrusive – a style almost as simple as the prattling of a child, and as warm and intimate as a mother's lullaby . . ."

December 29
A letter from Boyadzhiev in Sverdlovsk. The Central Red Army Theatre is going to do *Long, Long Ago*. Tikhon Khrennikov will write the music. Boyadzhiev asks whether there are any mistakes in the copies made by the Distribution Department and wants me to send corrections. I had no choice but to go to Pasternak to copy out the corrections in my only copy. I found him at work. I told him everything, not very coherently. He congratulated me and gave me back the play, after making me promise to return it as soon as I had done with it.

"How good that you at least are having some luck," he said, but immediately apologized for using the word "luck". "It is the wrong word – you have earned it a hundred times over." And he praised the play again.

December 31
Another long walk with Pasternak. He has a slight cold, and a touch of lumbago. As usual he talked at great length,

eagerly pouring out his words. There was splendid news on the radio today: our troops have taken Kerch and Feodosia. First we talked about this, and then about the war in general. He said that during all the months spent in Peredelkino and Moscow before leaving, and also during the first days here, he had been in an excellent mood because he had been placed by events on an equal footing with the rest of the world, he had become "like everybody else": firewatching on the roof in Lavrushinski Street,* sleeping out at his dacha next to the anti-aircraft guns – and all this "far away from the Soviet Government". He had thought that all the bureaucrats and "sergeant majors" might have been weeded out of literature by the general flight and panic, but it looked as though he was wrong: "I underestimated their adaptability, their phenomenal capacity for survival . . ." As we parted, he wished that the New Year might bring me "everything we have spoken about so much together, and, even more, what we have been silent about". I invited him to come and see the New Year in with me and my friends. At first he seemed to leap at the idea, saying he would be by himself that evening, since Zinaida Nikolayevna was at a party in the orphanage, and he even asked me for my friends' address, but then he remembered his lumbago and decided it might be better to stay at home. A curious point: he did not realize the Crimea had been occupied by the Germans, and was surprised when I told him.

"The future is the worst of all abstractions. The future never comes in the form you expect. Or wouldn't it be truer to say that it never in fact comes at all? If you expect X to happen and Y happens instead, how can you say it was what you expected? Everything that really exists does so only within the framework of the present. Even our feeling for the past comes to us from the present. Actually the past is also an abstraction, but a less artificial one than the future."

"A man has equal need of both reason and unreason, of

both calm and anxiety. Leave him only reason and calm, and he will become dull, colourless and lethargic. Give him only unreason and anxiety, and he will lose both himself and his world. The poet is a man of extremes: he seeks reason in unreason and calm in anxiety, unreason in reason, and anxiety in calm. Everybody has this inborn need to seek for opposites in all things – just as almost everybody is born with a rudimentary gift of poetry."

In the evening, before going to our party, I called on him for a moment to ask once again whether he would like to see the New Year in with us. He was lying in bed with a book of Victor Hugo. There was a small lamp on the table. That was how Pasternak spent New Year's Eve. Leonov and Fedin have been getting ready for several days and laid in all kinds of nice things to eat. But it obviously never even occurred to them to invite him. He again declined my invitation and repeated his good wishes.

January 2, 1942
We have thirty degrees of frost and strong winds. I ran into Fedin today and he told me that the Chistopol branch of the Union of Writers had been given the right to accept new members, subject to later confirmation by the official Secretariat in Kazan, and that Pasternak had suggested I should apply:

"Your play is doing very well and it is simply a disgrace that you are not yet a member of the Union. Boris Leonidovich spoke very highly of it . . ."

I sat down there and then, at a corner of Khesin's desk in the V.U.O.A.P., and wrote out my application and short curriculum vitae.

Fedin asked me to give the play to Trenev, who would then pass it on to Leonov and himself. I had been wanting to return it to Pasternak, but there was nothing to be done: I took it to Trenev. He greeted me rather dourly and I immediately regretted giving the manuscript to him.

January 9

I hear that at the last meeting of the Board of the Union of Writers (on Monday the 5th) my application for membership was accepted. My play had been read by Trenev and Leonov. The meeting was attended by Fedin, Leonov, Isakovski, Trenev, Aseyev, Pasternak and Dobrynin. Pasternak spoke warmly in my favour, and so did Trenev, contrary to expectation. Leonov also praised the play. I was accepted unanimously. The decision still has to be confirmed in Kazan by the Secretariat (Bakhmetyev, Apletin and others). In fact confirmation is a foregone conclusion, given the unquestionable authority of the people who have accepted my application. My first impulse was to go to Pasternak and thank him, but I resisted it. I don't want him to think I am imposing on him.

January 16

Met Pasternak on the staircase at V.U.O.A.P. He greeted me and asked why I was so thin. "I have been ill, and we are all living very badly at the moment." Next he said that he wanted to have a good talk with me. Everybody is very cheerful just now – things are going well at the front.

January 19

Met Pasternak in V.U.O.A.P. We talked about firewood and how to fetch it. It is terribly cold, and wood has to be brought up from the riverside. I told him the system for getting wood from *Litfund*. He listened carefully and then said: "I'm sorry, I don't understand it at all. Tell me again." I repeated it all somewhat disjointedly. He said I should visit him.

January 24

Went to see Pasternak this afternoon. It has never been so bitterly cold as in the last few days – on the 21st and 22nd it was 53 below zero in Chistopol, and 58 down by the river. Pasternak was sitting at his desk with a coat thrown over his shoulders – it is cold in his room. I apologized for interrupting while he was working, but he said he was only reading and was glad I had called . . .

"You don't read French, do you? Oh, of course, I've asked you that before . . . I wanted you to share the pleasure I get from Victor Hugo's book on Shakespeare. I am reading it a little at a time. It gives me so much to think about that I simply cannot read too much at a time. It is a treasure-house of ideas, not only about Shakespeare, but about art in general. It makes you feel like an ignorant child . . . I can't refrain from quoting a few bits for you . . ." (He read them out, translating at sight):

" 'To give every object as much space as it needs – neither more, nor less: that is simplicity in art. To be simple means to be equitable. That is the law of true taste. Each thing must be given its due place and expressed by its proper word. On the sole condition that there is a certain hidden balance and that a certain mysterious proportion is preserved, the greatest complexity in either style or composition may prove to be simplicity . . .' "

He stopped and looked at me triumphantly, as though inviting me to share his delight. I started to say something, but he interrupted:

"No, wait a moment. That's not all. Listen to this:
'The simplicity of poetry is like that of an oak with its spreading branches. Would you say that an oak tree strikes you as too Byzantine or elaborate? Its innumerable anti-theses: the massive trunk and tiny leaves, the hard bark and velvety moss; the light it drinks in and the shadow it casts; the branches used to crown heroes and the acorns fed to swine – are we really to believe all this speaks of artificiality, affectation and bad taste? Does it mean that the oak is rather too clever? That it is ludicrously mannered, afflicted by conceit and self-importance? Or that it belongs to the decadent school? Can it be that only a head of cabbage may

lay claim to simplicity?' "

Pausing to draw breath, Pasternak continued to read:

" 'In Shakespeare there is no self-restraint, no assuredness; there are no limits and no reticences. What is there, then? There is everything. Nothing is absent in him but absence itself. He holds nothing in reserve. He never abstains. He knows no barriers – like a luxuriant growth, like a sprouting seed, like the dawn of a new day, like a flame. If you are cold, you can warm your hands at this fire. He gives himself, bestows himself, lavishes himself, but never comes to the end of himself. He simply cannot be depleted. He lacks nothing except a limit. He fills himself up, spends himself, scatters himself around by the handful, by the spadeful, and then begins all over again. He is a kind of bottomless basket of the spirit from some fairytale . . . In the depths of his turbulence there is serenity, because his turbulence springs from humanity . . .' "

"You know, ever since I started working on my translations of Shakespeare, I have wanted to write something about him. Or rather, I did until I read this book of Hugo's. Now I simply would not dare. To think that it hasn't been translated here . . . No, you must listen to some more . . . I'm not boring you? Very well:

'Hamlet pretends to be mad not to make it easier to carry out his plan of revenge, but to save his life. The poet is also a magnificent historian who knew the ways of these baleful kingdoms. In those times it was woe betide the man who learned of a murder committed by a king. Voltaire surmises that Ovid was exiled from Rome because he knew something terrible about Augustus. To know that the king was a murderer was in itself a crime of high treason. A man suspected of suspecting it could count himself doomed.' "

P. next read out Hugo's description of Macbeth. I told him how once, during a conversation about the trials of

1937–8, Meyerhold had said: Read and re-read Macbeth.

P. gave a gasp, was silent for a moment, and said then: "No, let's not talk about that – it's too terrible" – and after another pause: "You see how alive he is, Shakespeare: always putting terrifying associations into our heads . . ." He then quoted Victor Hugo's remarks about Shakespeare's "double effect".

We spoke about his translations. His attitude is a model of how a writer should approach something not part of his life's work but which he has to do as a matter of necessity: once he has started, he forces himself to get genuinely carried away by it.

January 28

Another of the regular "literary Wednesdays" at the Teachers' Club. Aseyev read parts of his new long poem, still unfinished, and some new lyrics. It was all rather shallow and rhetorical – apart from two minor items, one about a dragonfly on the barrel of a rifle, and another called "Conversation with a Friend" – but everybody showered him with compliments, some (like Pasternak) out of kindheartedness and others (Arski, V. Bokov, Nikitin and others) out of poor taste. Pasternak made a long speech about art which it is almost impossible to put down even in summary form. It consisted entirely of the most subtle paradoxes, a firework display of brilliant thoughts following each other in no particular sequence. It was all beautifully spoken, with youthful passion and an engaging warmth of spirit. He was actually presiding at the gathering. For some reason the writers were outnumbered by wives today, and Pasternak was concerned that they should all be comfortably seated – he kept running out to fetch chairs from the reading-room and ushering them to their places. It was cold in the room, but he took off his outer coat, setting an example to everybody else. Before the proceedings began, he went over to Zinaida Nikolayevna several times – she was sitting huddled in her coat by the iron stove – and spoke to her very gently, trying to coax her into doing something, and calling her tenderly "my pet". All during Aseyev's reading, he smiled, nodded with delight, and kept saying quietly (but clearly enough to be heard) "very good", "splendid", and in general behaved with extraordinary graciousness, like a perfect host. I could not take my eyes off him – he was a thousand times more magnificent than Aseyev's poems. He is so handsome and natural – a poet in the true sense of the word. Everything he said was infinitely full of meaning and complex – a shorthand record of his thoughts:

"A poet's main gift is imagination. A rich, boisterous, unruly imagination is what distinguished Mayakovski and Yesenin from all the non-poets who were merely expert with words. It is imagination that gives the freedom, the daring and the boldness without which there are no victories in poetry . . ."

"No one can give me freedom as a gift if I do not already possess it in embryo within myself. Nothing is more spurious than outer freedom if one lacks inner freedom. A citizen of Chicago or some such place, chewing over the fare provided by his newspaper or radio set, is actually less free than a philosopher in the solitary confinement of a prison cell . . ."

"Getting to know oneself is not an exercise with a foregone conclusion. You have to take risks. Taking spiritual risks is the professional duty of a poet – or rather, it's the medium in which he works, like height for a steeplejack, minefields for a sapper or the bottom of the sea for a diver . . ."

"In art you have to be yourself only to the extent to which you cannot help it anyway. You should no more have to worry about it than you do about your fingernails growing – not a good comparison, but please try to understand me. You are born as yourself, and then you lose yourself, and

66

spend all your life trying to get back to what you were . . .
You must take on tasks which are beyond your strength –
in the first place, because you only acquire strength while
going about something you think is beyond you."

February 2

I was talking with Pasternak about the war when he suddenly
fell silent and looked lost in thought, and then, quite unexpectedly, he asked: "You couldn't lend me fifteen roubles
for a day or two, could you?" Fortunately I had that much
on me. He took the money, thanked me, but then abruptly
pulled out his wallet again and started handing the money
back to me.

"No, I can't borrow from you. You're not Pogodin."

"But it's not a couple of thousand, it's only fifteen."

"Yes, I know, but . . ." (debating with himself) "you see,
I'm in such a jam over money at the moment . . . All right,
I'll take it . . . But no, I can't – you're very poor and you
need it yourself, don't you?"

"But no, Boris Leonidovich, I can manage."

"No, no, I know very well you don't live like Fedin or
Leonov."

"But you wouldn't think of asking *them*, whereas we are on
the same footing in this and it's natural for you to borrow
from me."

"Very well, I'll take it then. I do need it badly. How
stupid – having to borrow fifteen roubles. Thank you!"

We both felt very embarrassed and awkward.

Leonov once told me he regarded Pushkin's *The Captain's
Daughter* as the greatest achievement in world literature. I
was taken aback by this, particularly as nothing could be
further from Leonov's own work. I mentioned to Pasternak
how puzzling I found it:

"No, no, I understand very well what he means. You
cannot imitate what you love the best. But it is a remarkable
thing to admit, and you're quite right – it seems strange at
first that he should say not Dostoyevski or Leskov, but

Pushkin. But it tells you everything about Leonov: this is his opposite pole – and we all gravitate spiritually to our opposite pole. Leonov's first love was probably Dostoyevski. Pushkin represents his inner maturity – but he is remote from him in his writing."

I find it odd that P. scarcely reads the papers; it's not that he's by any means indifferent to what is happening at the front, and he rejoices at the good news we have been hearing so often recently. But he doesn't go to read the newspapers in the Party reading-room, and never hurries over to hear the latest news bulletin on the loudspeaker:

"I always get to know the important things anyway – you tell me about them, for instance . . . In the present state of the world one must be sparing in one's intake of information, otherwise one may be dazed and stupefied by it. Your existence becomes illusory if, instead of getting down to work in the morning, you just wait for news and live on the echoes of things happening elsewhere . . . No, I don't mean it's a bad thing – some people find they need it, perhaps, but I just don't. I have to work every day, or I feel ashamed of myself."

He is indeed a remarkable worker, but he never gives the appearance of doing some burdensome and essential chore – he works in the same way that others relax; he works because it's necessary, but also because he enjoys it – this aspect may even be the main one. The only thing after the categorical imperative "one must work" is the choice of *what* to do. At the moment he is translating *Romeo and Juliet* and while resting or out walking he talks endlessly of Shakespeare. He is interested in everything about him. He finds it ludicrous that anybody should doubt the authorship of the actor at the Globe theatre. In this connection he talks of the miracle of an artist's development, of the kind of genius that Goethe referred to as "anticipation" – that is, an artist's ability to know even things that he has not personally experienced. As proof of Shakespeare's authenticity he mentions the

68

inconsistencies and repetitions one finds in the plays: "Fakes are always much more carefully done than a genuine article." He speaks of Shakespeare's gift for improvisation, by virtue of which the conventional and frequently borrowed plots were subordinated to a soaring poetic fancy: "I have now been through two of his masterpieces with very close attention to the text and I can tell you that there is no question of more than one hand – they were written by one man whom you can almost hear breathing . . ." Pasternak believes Shakespeare found it easier to improvise in verse than to write in prose. He even thinks Shakespeare did first drafts in verse of scenes that he later re-wrote in prose.

An observation on the special quality of the general education in the humanities which then started with Latin: "In those days boys picked up Latin and classical mythology in the same way that the youth of today learns all about how a motorcar works." . . . "Shakespeare always wrote at great speed and probably never re-read a play once it was no longer put on. He forgot what he had written and knew less about his own work than any modern research student writing a dissertation on him."

February 4

At today's "literary Wednesday" in the Teachers' Club, the young poet Yakov Keihaus was billed to read his translations. It was bitterly cold with a blizzard blowing. Apart from the poet himself, only old Pavel Arski, Hugo Huppert and myself turned up. Keihaus, very poorly dressed and consumptive-looking, is a tall young fellow with an Assyrian type of beard and a green scarf wrapped round his thin neck. As we were wondering what to do, and thinking of putting the reading off to another evening, Pasternak suddenly appeared in a very animated state, red-cheeked from the cold, full of friendly concern and eloquent apologies for being late, whereupon Keihaus said he would be glad to read to us.

He recited his version of Heine's "Bimini" and several very good translations of poems by Kipling on historical themes. Pasternak listened with visible pleasure and said he would like to hear the rather lengthy "Bimini" again. Keihaus went pink with joy. Pasternak listened with a smile and at the end praised the translation very much. He said he would like to hear some original verse. Apologizing for the gloominess of his subject-matter, Keihaus read out the prologue and several further extracts from his long poem "A Night in Solitude" about October 16 in Moscow, evacuation and war. Then he read three poems about his son, the second of which Pasternak liked very much and asked him to repeat. He said he liked Keihaus's poems because they had arisen "not through rhythmic or verbal inertia, but as cognitive responses to the world". The poor poet was in the seventh heaven. I enjoyed this evening very much more than the one with Aseyev last week. I saw Pasternak home and on the way I listened to his discursive monologues of which, as usual, I am able to reconstruct only a small part . . . He is very upset that a reading from his completed translation of *Romeo and Juliet*, which was to have taken place next Wednesday, has been put off because of a Pushkin anniversary meeting now planned for that evening. He says it will be his birthday on the 11th (29th Old Style) and that he would, therefore, have particularly liked to read on that day. His disappointment is very great, and quite spontaneous, like a child's. We were accompanied as far as the square by Hugo Huppert, the emigré German poet and excellent translator of Mayakovski. The other day the newspapers published a message to the German people signed by a group of German writers and other public figures, including Huppert. I asked how they had managed to get his signature from him here in Chistopol, and it turned out that he knew nothing at all about it until I told him! He laughed and said he would go and read it in the Party reading-room first thing tomorrow morning.

February 10

Went out walking with Pasternak. At first we talked about his work on the Shakespeare translations, and then about many other things. Some of it I remember and can put down:

"My translation of *Romeo and Juliet* is different from *Hamlet.* I am trying to be simpler, conveying the sense of untranslatable figures of speech or popular sayings instead of supplying equivalent images . . ."

"I think the best Russian translations of *Romeo and Juliet* are Mikhailov's in Gerbel's four-volume edition, and also Apollon Grigoryev's – although this suffers from an excessive 'Russification' of the original. To my mind the most beautiful part of the play is Act Five . . ."

"I shall never forget the air-raid on Moscow during the night of July 23 and the red glow of fires in the summer sky in the morning. I was on the roof all night and two days later I read an account of the whole thing in *Izvestia* by a colleague who had spent the night in the cellar . . ." ("Downright dishonesty!" I interjected) – "No, no – he wasn't being dishonest, he was just doing the best he could. I don't blame him, but the demand for this kind of newspaper story . . ."

"The good thing about life in Chistopol is that we're less shielded from the elements than in Moscow: we feel daunted by the bitter cold and rejoice when the thaw comes – man's normal relations with nature are restored. And even the lack of amenities – such things as water-taps and electric fixtures – doesn't strike me personally as a hardship, and I think I can say this almost in the name of poetry . . ."

"In Peredelkino, just before coming here, I was trying to do as much work as possible, to earn some money, and I often sat down to write during the night while air-raids were going on. The air-raids themselves didn't trouble me – it was even quieter round about – but I was very much put out by our servant, an elderly, sensible woman, but a fearful coward. She kept bursting into the room and startling me with her bloodcurdling shrieks: 'They are shooting again! Oh my God!' and then she would run off to hide somewhere and I had to chase after her to close the door which she left wide open, breaking the blackout regulations . . ."

"I have a nice room with lots of light, but I can only get warm by keeping the door open to the next room, where the people of the house live – but all day long they are either quarrelling, doing school lessons, gossiping or putting on gramophone records, and I can't help hearing it all. Even when I'm hard at work, only half my mind is on it, while the other half is on the neighbours. But even so, I produce much more here than in Moscow – though I am not so sure about the quality . . ."

"The salvation of real art from the steady advance of bogus art – much more to be feared than incomprehension or indifference – is not to be found in working harder at it. Art is inconceivable without risk, without spiritual self-sacrifice, without freedom and boldness of imagination. Real art always comes as a surprise. You cannot foresee the unpredictable, or regulate the unruly . . ."

"Have you noticed the similarity between Tolstoi's language and Lenin's? When Italy invaded Abyssinia *Izvestia* published some extracts from Tolstoi's diary about Italy's first attack on Abyssinia in the mid-1890's. When I read them, I was literally shaken by the resemblance which now suddenly struck me. Perhaps I am overdoing it, but I attach great importance to this likeness – quite astonishing in the intonation, in the bluntness with which both of them denounce the demure, conventional commonplaces of a narrow-mindedly middle-class colonialist civilization. For me this resemblance points to something deep in the national character, something that always appears inopportune, or irrelevant to the course of ordinary daily life. It is just this in Tolstoi – his tempestuous diatribes and unceremonious plainspeaking – that I now feel to be an expression of our national temperament, and also what he has in common with Lenin. I see here the beginning of the tradition which might, if you wish, be called 'Socialist Realism' – if it were not that this phrase now so often masks quite the reverse: everything that is empty, high-flown, rhetorical, without substance, useless in human terms, and morally suspect . . ."

"In order to exist evil must masquerade as good. The pretence alone makes it immoral. One may say that evil always has an inferiority complex: it does not dare to be frank. Intellectuals of Nietzsche's kind thought the chief trouble about evil was just this – its sense of inferiority, its propensity to disguise itself as its opposite. They believed that evil only had to fly its true colours for it to become moral. But evil cannot do this: even the Nazis have to dress up the blackest of their crimes – racism – in various arguments about its benefits to the German people."

"I like only one of Nietzsche's ideas. Somewhere he says: 'Your true essence lies not deep within you, but out of reach high above you.' This is almost Christianity . . ."

"I have Jewish blood in my veins, but nothing is more alien to me than Jewish nationalism – except, perhaps, Great-Russian chauvinism. On this issue I'm all for complete Jewish assimilation, and personally I only feel at home in Russian culture, with its wide range of influences, as did Pushkin . . ."

"Once, in the mid-twenties, I turned up at one of those regular mass rallies of poets feeling lost, inwardly confused,

73

dissatisfied with myself, and unworthy of anybody's attention, but when I came out onto the stage of the Polytechnic,* I was greeted by loud applause. At that moment I realized how easily I could embark on a new career – one revolting in its cheapness and tawdry glitter. And there and then I felt repelled for ever more by the limelight, by this wantonness fit almost for a variety show. I saw it as my task to revive the idea of poetry printed in books, on pages which speak with the power of deafening silence. Instead of the poetry-reading trips of others, I preferred the kind of journeys made by Pushkin, Lermontov and Tiutchev through their books, and I have devoted all my strength to the rigours of journeys such as these, which have utterly absorbed me and are so unlike the easy victories of travelling stage-performers . . . What about Mayakovski, you ask? I began to marvel at his genius before most of the people who now swear by him, and for a long time I loved him to the point of worship. Mayakovski embodied such a live and shattering truth on the stage, and gave so much that for several generations to come he vindicated the use of this forum (which was unquestionably for him alone) and thereby redeemed in advance the sins of all later stars of the poetic music-hall, which has now developed into something quite barbaric."

February 15
It's not so cold now. During the day the sun even thawed the snow a little and icicles have formed. The roads smell slightly of horse droppings, as in one's childhood. Tomorrow is the first day of Lent, as Pasternak told me when I ran into him today. I was carrying a book on Nikolai Gué, the painter, which I had just borrowed from the library. It was about this that our conversation began:

"I knew Gué when I was a boy. He sometimes even used to say that he had two real friends: Tolstoi and me. I was then five years old. For me he wasn't a famous painter, but an old friend of my father's – simply 'Uncle Kolia' . . ."

74

As usual, we walked down to the Kama, and talked about various things:

"Many people take me for something different from what I am. It was this that poisoned my relations with Gorki until the end of his life. In Peredelkino Fadeyev sometimes used to come and see me and after a few drinks he would begin to take me into his confidence. I was embarrassed and upset that he felt he could do this with me, of all people . . . Fadeyev is well disposed to me personally, but if he received orders to have me hung, drawn and quartered he would carry them out conscientiously and make his report without batting an eyelid – though the next time he got drunk he would say how sorry he was for me and what a splendid fellow I had been. We talk about people having 'a split personality', and there are many such in this country. But in Fadeyev's case I would put it differently: his personality is divided off into a number of watertight sections, like a submarine. Only alcohol breaks down the bulkheads and mixes everything up together . . ."

"If ever I had to bring out my collected works, I would be ruthless about my early ones. To be absolutely frank, my collected works are still to be written – though I suppose I might already have just about enough for a single volume. But no more, no more, I swear to you. And please don't think I'm just being coy. God forbid! This is my deepest conviction: for several decades now I've been living on credit and have still not done anything really worthwhile. I am not afraid of such thoughts – they could be frightening only to a spiritual bankrupt, but for me they are simply a challenge."

"I am gradually beginning to find translation irksome, but everything else is precarious, alas – at least I can be sure of making some sort of a living out of it. *Hamlet* is my best piece of work – this I know, whatever people may say about it. *Hamlet* has never been translated like this before. It is the most subjective of all Shakespeare's tragedies – as far as a tragedy can be subjective. *Romeo and Juliet* is a different thing again. In the text of *Romeo and Juliet* I have found many almost word-for-word resemblances to Mayakovski's imagery – including 'love's boat' smashed on the reefs of life in Romeo's final lines.* The similarity is so close here that I had to tone it down, so it wouldn't be too obvious. There is no doubt at all in my mind that Mayakovski read Shakespeare and learned from him. They even have a natural or innate, as it were, affinity – in the style of their wit, for example.

Mayakovski's literary pedigree is much more complicated than people imagine. I see him as a descendant of Dostoyevski. His early verse could have been written by Dostoyevski's younger characters – youthful rebels such as Hyppolite, Raskolnikov and the hero of *A Raw Youth*. All his best things are said with absolute finality, in a take-it-or-leave-it manner – and not even said, but flung with extraordinary vehemence in the teeth of society, the city, the world at large . . ."

I asked him why he had stopped work on the long novel of which extracts had appeared in *Literary Gazette* and *30 Days* in 1938:

"I found it very hard to write this novel because of the way the attitude to the First World War changes with twists and turns in the political line . . ."

February 20
This morning I had just sat down to work, as usual, when there was suddenly a tap on the window. I looked up, saw it was Pasternak and ran outside. He didn't want to come in and asked me to go on a walk with him. I went back in to put on my coat while he waited, knocking icicles off the eaves.

"Here I am," he said, "already going grey, but the icicles

are just the same as when I was a child. I think I even remember that one up there . . ."

We went our usual way down past the cathedral to the Kama, and then towards the creek on the right.

I have heard from my mother that there are already posters up in Moscow advertising the première of my new play, and I told him. He congratulated me heartily.

It has been a nice day, almost like spring, and we had an interesting conversation, of which I am putting down a small part here. It began with Pasternak saying that whenever he sees the ice-bound barges on the Kama he always thinks of Marina Tsvetayeva who said just before leaving here that she would rather freeze into the ice of the Kama in Chistopol than go away:

"Actually, winter was still far off, even though people were already thinking of it with dread, and the barges were sailing endlessly down the river, one after another . . . I loved her very much and now I am sorry I didn't seek the opportunity to tell her so as often as she needed, perhaps, to hear it. Her life was a heroic one. Every day she performed some act of bravery. These acts were out of loyalty to the only country of which she was a citizen: poetry . . .

Of course, she was more Russian than any of us – not only by blood, but also in the rhythms that dwelled in her soul, in her tremendous language, unequalled in its power . . .

We all wrote badly in our youth, but with me this stage went on far too long, since I am in general a slow developer: everything comes to me later. Marina went through her imitative phase very quickly and very early. Even at that period of life when all one's mistakes and lapses are forgivable and even have their charm, she was already an accomplished poet of rare power and sureness of touch.

I feel guilty at not having tried to dissuade her from returning to the Soviet Union when I could have done.* What was there for her here? She was a pauper in Paris, and she died a pauper here. But here there was even worse

77

in store: the senseless, unspeakable tragedy of the destruction of all her dear ones – about which I don't yet have the courage to speak . . ."

I asked him who was to blame that after her return here she found herself so lonely and homeless – which was what, in effect, led to her death in Yelabuga.

Without a moment's thought he replied: "I am!" and then added: "We all are. I and the others. I and Aseyev, and Fedin and Fadeyev. All of us . . . We were full of pious intentions, but did nothing, consoling ourselves with the thought that there was nothing we could do. We and the State. It can do everything, and we can do nothing. Once again we agreed there was nothing we could do, and just went off to dinner. Most of us suffered no loss of appetite. It was our common crime, the consequence of our spiritual deafness, of our lack of conscience, and criminal egotism . . . One day I will write about her, I have already begun – in verse and in prose. I have been wanting to do it for a long time, but I am still holding back – to gather the strength needed to do justice to the theme, that is, to her: Marina. To write about her you must bring all your powers of expression to bear."

[Next, by an obvious association of ideas, we talked about Stalin and the question which so preoccupied people in the thirties and forties: did Stalin himself know about all the crimes of his repressive régime? Needless to say, I recorded this part of the conversation in a very abbreviated and camouflaged form. After a brief pause for thought Pasternak said:

"If he knows nothing, then that is also a crime – perhaps the greatest of which a leader can be guilty . . ."

He went on to speak of Stalin as "a giant of the pre-Christian era of human history".* I asked whether he had perhaps meant to say "of the *post*-Christian era", but he insisted on the way he had put it and gave his reasons at great length. But I did not put any of this down.]

He complained about not having been able to work the last few days – which was why he had gone out for a walk today, and "so prevented you from working as well."

"I know", he went on, "that it's nothing to do with all the hindrances I blame it on, but that it's my own fault. You will always find any number of things to get in the way when you don't *want* to work. This is rare in my case, and I don't like to force myself. If you try to drive yourself beyond a certain point, the work may lose the appeal without which something will be missing, even if you do it all as you had planned . . . In those periods of my life when I worked mainly at night, I trained myself not to think of work during the day so that I could always return fresh to what I had written and already half-forgotten. But even not working or indulging in various forms of idleness was also a kind of preparation for work. After sitting up all night you feel drowsy and inert, and in this haze of torpor a very important preliminary stage of your work takes place – you begin to hanker after activity, you long for everything to achieve its final and definitive form, and what you have already completed goes through significant modifications. Your work, in fact, never actually stops, but simply continues in a different form – invisibly instead of openly. All this, of course, applies mainly to the writing of one's own poetry. I do my translating work in a more – what shall I say? – rational, or sober way . . ."

I don't remember what it was that got us on to the subject of the theatre. He is very much drawn to it at the moment. It may also be that he is so interested in me because I am a "man of the theatre", a pupil of Meyerhold and a playwright. From the way he talks about it I sense that he thinks it is an important form of art because of the immediacy of its impact, its aura of success. As a member of the audience in the theatre he is remarkably spontaneous in his reactions. Recently, when I went to the tiny local theatre to a performance of *Somebody Else's Baby** I saw him laughing so much that he almost fell off his chair. I was rather astonished

– this type of humour strikes me as pretty unsophisticated. He often says he dreams of writing a play and his interest in my work is of course connected with the fact that drama is now at the focal point of his own interests.

His friendship with Meyerhold certainly does not mean that his own tastes extend no further than the "Left" theatre – he speaks respectfully of the Arts Theatre and seems not yet to have lost hope of seeing his beloved *Hamlet* put on there.

February 23
Went to evening celebrating Red Army Day. Incident with Pasternak.* Strolled around with him afterwards. He was upset and embarrassed.

February 26
Today at the Teachers' Club Pasternak read from his translation of *Romeo and Juliet*. Tickets were sold at 4 and 5 roubles – to buy gifts for Red Army soldiers. The town's electricity station broke down in the early evening and all the lights went off. Pasternak read by the light of two paraffin lamps. The hall was practically full – all the writers' colony and many of the local intelligentsia were there – even though *The Precipice** was opening at the theatre in the Cultural Centre next door. The reading was only half-an-hour late in beginning.

Pasternak wore a black suit and a colourful knitted tie, and had white felt boots on his feet. He was genial and relaxed. As usual before his readings, he started with some introductory remarks, but wandered from the point, skipping from one thing to another, until he lost his way altogether and stopped short. He read not very well but engagingly, in a loud clear manner. He is absolutely not an actor, and when he tries to put some expression into the character parts (such as the nurse), it just sounds naive. He managed Romeo and Lorenzo best of all. The scene of Mercutio's death came over in all its drama. The translation itself is very good, almost better than *Hamlet*. The rhymed passages are done in exemplary fashion.

He did not read the whole text but cut out some of the minor scenes. He told us at the beginning that he thought the fifth act was the most beautiful of all, but that we should "have to be patient" before we got to it. He read the whole of it. Whenever he left anything out in the other acts he summarized it in his own words and sometimes – also very typical of him – the summary together with his comments grew to such proportions that, suddenly checking himself, he would say with a laugh: "Ah well, I suppose it might be simpler just to read it." There was a short interval after the third act and everything was over by a quarter to eleven. Somebody said he wanted to see me, so I went over to him. With many apologies he returned my fifteen roubles.

February 27
Went out for a walk with G. O. Vinokur and after the usual conversation about the war, he started talking about Pasternak. Vinokur made the very true remark that Pasternak is a living contradiction of the common idea that booklearning is incompatible with a spontaneous poetic vision of the world. Nothing comes amiss to a real poet. If Pasternak were not so well-read, would the range of his associations be so wide and unexpected? Goethe, Byron, Pushkin, Fet and Blok were all highly educated, but this only made their poetic gifts all the richer. We talked about the relations between Pasternak and Aseyev, and Vinokur said he is reminded of Pushkin and Baratynski. Aseyev suffers from the same "Salieri complex"* as Baratynski. Vinokur, who knew Mayakovski well, confirmed Lily Brik's story that Mayakovski was always murmuring Pasternak's verse to himself. He loved Pasternak as one might love a disobedient younger brother who had revolted against one's own irksome tutelage.

I asked G.O. to explain a strange phrase Pasternak used recently when he told me that the Briks' apartment was "virtually a branch of the Moscow militia". G.O. grinned and said nothing, but then – emphasizing that he was giving only his personal opinion, etc. – began to tell me about the Briks' friendship with the famous Jan Agranov, a leading Chekist who took an interest in literary matters.

Agranov began as head of a special department in the GPU and the NKVD* and then became deputy people's commissar. He perished in 1937 (as I remember people saying, he threw himself out of a window when they came for him). Agranov and his wife were often at the Brikses. G.O. himself had met him there. It was thanks to his all-powerful influence that Mayakovski was allowed to go abroad so often, but after Mayakovski had fallen in love with Tatyana Yakovleva in Paris and wanted to go back there to her in the autumn of 1929, he was refused a visa. The Briks were possibly worried about Mayakovski marrying an emigrée and no doubt informed Agranov. Mayakovski was terribly upset at being denied a visa for the first time in his life. An innocent by nature, he simply couldn't take in or accept the idea that he, Mayakovski, was not trusted. This was the beginning of the inner drama which ended in his suicide. G.O. does not think the worst construction need be put on it: in their own eyes the Briks may have been right in trying to protect Mayakovski from what they felt was a dangerous infatuation, but even so, there was something sinister about Agranov's part in the business. Pasternak was probably thinking about this episode, which was known to Mayakovski's friends.

G.O. was close to LEF,* published in it, and was friendly with the Briks and Mayakovski. He is a clever and very decent man, and has excellent taste.

March 3
Today I was queuing for bread in what used to be our *Litfund* restaurant which long ago stopped serving meals because of lack of supplies and has now been turned into a kind of special store for us. The queue was quite long –

mostly writers' wives or the servants which some of them still have. Pasternak came in and people shouted at him rudely to close the door. He apologized, very embarrassed. I waved to him as he took his place modestly at the end of the queue. He smiled at me but didn't understand that I wanted him to have my turn. I tried to take his ration cards, but he started explaining something to me and the queue got restless — "No, you really mustn't! Why?", he protested, still smiling. It was nearly my turn already, but I left my place and stood near him. Everybody gave us odd looks and we started talking about Apollon Grigoryev. I don't believe he really understood my purpose in standing next to him and simply thought I wanted to chat. But people do have a conscience after all — when it was my turn, they called me up to the counter and Pasternak as well. It was all done in such a nice, friendly fashion that he couldn't refuse. Everybody smiled and looked pleased for some reason. But with a loaf of bread in his *avoska** he just went on talking as eloquently as before about Apollon Grigoryev and the early days of *The Muscovite*.

March 5

M. Nikitin read passages from his book at our "literary Wednesday". It is a muddled, high-flown and far-fetched piece of writing. The discussion was much superior to the object of it. The speakers were: Pasternak, Leonov, Aseyev, Lerman, Dobrynin, and a few others besides. Everybody spoke in general terms, managing in various ways to steer clear of any direct expression of opinion about the work. After several such contributions I left before the end and went out into the reading-room. Vinokur was sitting there and listening to the first performance of Shostakovich's Seventh Symphony which was being relayed over the radio from Kuibyshev. I was in time for the third and fourth movements. The discussion ended almost at the same time as the broadcast, and Pasternak and I left the building together. I saw him home. The frost was getting harder.

There is nothing more splendid than to walk over the snow when it crunches under your feet. Pasternak wanted to know what I thought of his reading of *Romeo and Juliet* and then asked me laughingly where he could get hold of a flue pipe for his samovar. When I told him about the Shostakovich broadcast, he chided me for not calling him out.

Today he talked about how "the faceless is more complicated than a face", but he developed this old idea of his (expressed already in *Safe Conduct*) on rather different lines. I told him of Meyerhold's dictum that "simplicity is the apex, not the starting point", and he was quite delighted by it:

"Nothing is more complicated than chaos. Art overcomes chaos, just as Christianity overcame all the vast agglomerations of pre-historic time. The chaos of pre-history does not know the phenomenon of memory: memory is history, and memory is art. The past does not exist outside memory and comes to us only through memory. Both history and art are thus children of the same mother – memory. Art simplifies by elevation, not by reduction; it is reality crystallized out of chaos – which, by its very nature, is the opposite of reality and, though present, does not exist, or rather, exists only by virtue of art and history, by virtue of faces arising to challenge its facelessness . . ."

I butted in to quote Herzen's words: "What you do not dare to utter only half-exists."

"Oh yes, yes, that's true. It seems to contradict Tiutchev's famous aphorism,* but in fact these are simply two sides of the same coin . . ."

We were already standing in front of his house. As he said goodbye, he asked me whether tomorrow I could bring him *Long, Long Ago* and promised to finish reading it straight away.

March 6
I took my play along to Pasternak in the afternoon. I did

not stay long. There is hard frost again in Chistopol. He asked me to look in again tomorrow and promised to read the whole thing today. Soviet troops have taken Yukhnov. It is now the custom during our meetings that I tell him the latest military and political news.

Turning over the pages of my play, he suddenly said: "Your masterstroke is to have chosen such a worthy and captivating subject. When I read the first two acts I suddenly felt as though I had found a box with all my favourite childhood toys in some dark attic."

March 7

Talked for almost five hours with Pasternak at his lodgings and came home drunk with happiness. He has not finished reading the play, and the conversation was about other things, but infinitely fascinating . . .

I arrived, all spruced up, just after noon. He was washing in his room and shouted to me to wait a moment in the kitchen. The pudgy landlady was standing there with her children next to the paraffin stove. There was a poster of the film *Song of Love* on the wall. You could hear the cheerful sound of water splashing and loud spluttering noises from Pasternak. At last he opened the door and invited me in. He was in trousers and a crumpled white vest splashed with water. He continued to dress as he talked, buttoning up his shirt, putting on his collar, braces and jacket. The lowest button on the right side of his jacket hung by a thread, and I couldn't take my eyes off it. The floor was flooded with water. He got a brush and mopped up. He made me take a seat but it was twenty minutes before he settled down himself and sat on the bed. I again examined the room when he went out for a moment. It is of medium size and the walls have been painted white after a fashion. There is a decorative pattern with black and red birds going all the way round them in the middle. There are two beds placed together (I recognized these as *Litfund* ones, the same as in the orphanage – I have one too), the table at which he

writes, and several chairs. Something passing for a cupboard
stands in one corner. It is all very uncomfortable, but there
is plenty of light. On the table there is a pile of large sheets
of paper – this is the manuscript of his *Romeo and Juliet* – an
old, two-volume edition of Shakespeare in the original, an
English dictionary, a French dictionary. There is Victor
Hugo's book on Shakespeare with many slips of paper
sticking out to mark places, and underneath it a thick
exercise-book full of quotations – probably from Hugo –
in Pasternak's handwriting. Also on the table are an ink-
well, a few pencils, some razor-blades, a heap of old letters
and receipts.

There is already some grey in his hair, but it does not
predominate. His eyes are an amber-brown colour, he has
strong face muscles, and a fresh complexion. One of his
upper front teeth is missing. He is sprightly and vigorous.

I find it very hard to put down our conversation. It was
always so much easier for me to write down what Meyerhold
said. Pasternak is prolix, discursive and chaotic – though
everything he says has its inner logic and only the form is
impressionistic or paradoxical. When he is groping for words,
he makes a strange, mooing kind of sound and his monologues are always punctuated by it.

"You said I overpraised Aseyev's latest verse. I have
been thinking about this. Perhaps you are right, but I
praised it partly because I wanted to encourage the feeling
of inner independence which he has begun to regain only
after many years here in Chistopol, now he is far away from
his editors and all the intrigues in the Union of Writers.
For a number of years I felt distant from him because of
the atmosphere in LEF and particularly because of the
Briks. One day the biographers will show what a disastrous
influence they had on Mayakovski. Aseyev is a very complex
man. A little while ago, here in Chistopol, he insulted me for
no reason at all, and even forced me to complain to Fedin
about him. What you call my 'overpraise' of him is probably

explained by a desire to overcome my resentment and dislike of him, which I do not want to go on rankling inside me . . .

It is always to take refuge in their own mediocrity that people herd together – whatever their platform may be: Nietzscheanism, Marxism, or Solovyev-type Christianity. Anybody who loves the truth and is searching for it is bound to feel constrained in marching ranks of whatever kind, wherever they may be marching to . . ."

"I find it odd that many of the writers living here moan and complain and fail to appreciate the great boon of inner independence that evacuation has given them. I am sure I shall always be grateful to Chistopol for this if for nothing else . . ."

"My position as a writer is not what it seems . . . Why do you smile? It's true: I am esteemed for more than I have actually done. I am terribly in arrears, and with all my fame I often feel like Khlestakov."* (This was said with undisguised sorrow.) "Sometimes I think of myself as a kind of phantom. Whenever I am in the company of people so imperturbably sure of themselves as Fedin, Leonov and others, I feel very peculiar indeed. On the one hand, I seem to have some kind of literary reputation – even abroad – but on the other I live with the constant, nagging sense of being almost an impostor. What have I achieved? What have any of us achieved? We have inherited this extraordinary Russian culture but we have traded it away and have nothing to show in return but hackwork and doggerel.

I would give a lot to be the author of *The Rout** or *Cement.** Yes, I would – don't look at me with such astonishment and don't misunderstand me: what I mean to say is that major works of literature exist only in association with a large readership . . ."

"We are all still waiting for the great works of our age.

I am sure that even Fedin and Leonov must feel their inadequacy . . . When I say 'we', I always have in mind those of us who proceed from continuity and tradition . . ."

"I have been translating for the last six years. It is really high time I did something of my own . . . 80% of your good opinion of me must be due to my translation of *Hamlet* – now don't deny it or I'll be upset . . . I've long thought all the rest far too complicated, forced and mannered" – at this I felt bound to protest – "No, no, no, don't say that – I am quite convinced of it. Don't force me to think badly of you, don't say that you love the 'early Pasternak'! What? You do love him? So much the worse for you. Then you are not going to like what I am proposing to do next. You will part company from me, as I did from Mayakovski in the twenties. The history of literature shows that every poet has different generations of readers who accept one but not another period in his work. Remember how it was with Pushkin, Tolstoi and Gorki. A writer must have the courage to disregard the tastes of his admirers, to fly in the face of their instinctive desire to force him to go on repeating himself. There is no greater sign of courage in a writer than to wake up one morning a pauper, free of everything. In this sense it is more important for an artist to lose than to find. The reader is always more conservative than the poet. Yes, even one like you. I hope I haven't hurt your feelings?"

"There is nothing more beneficial for the health than straightforwardness, candour, sincerity and an easy conscience. If I were a doctor I would write a study on the danger of habitual duplicity to physical health. It is worse than alcoholism . . ."

"To speak the truth one must be a heretic. This is how it was and will be in every age . . ."

"Our earlier literary allegiances, even though left behind

by the development of our taste, still go on living in us, refusing to die. For a long time now I have preferred Pushkin to Lermontov, Chekhov to Dostoyevski and even to Tolstoi, but once I am alone with myself, pen in hand, the law of the literary impulse – whose force is triple that of the original appeal – brings back into my writing the shades of their images, their technical devices, their rhythms and colours . . ."

"An urge to maintain the purity of a genre is the mark of the imitator. Pioneers and founders of schools always mix different elements of style and composition in barbaric fashion, conquering not by the laws of accepted taste, but by the promptings of intuition. And these lawless victories later serve as models for new throngs of imitators . . ."

"You must know how to surrender to what seems like idleness, to indulge in it without either forcing yourself or feeling guilty about it. The need for such idleness comes more often than not from an instinctive wish to leap over some difficult hurdle in the so-called subconscious – a hurdle you couldn't take in your stride in working hours. How often I have crossed such barriers unconsciously and with astonishing ease once I stopped trying and simply sank into idleness, into a sudden lethargy."

"On the rare occasions when I go to meetings at our Union of Writers and listen to the speeches of my colleagues – who are probably not a bit worse than myself – I am always reminded, for some reason, of *The Fruits of Enlightenment** with all that oratory of the kind you once heard from lawyers at banquets, the high-flown, puffed-up, banal way of holding forth which has become habitual or even obligatory."

"You cannot tell me that we ourselves are completely without blame for all the bad things around us. The atmosphere of public life is not created from scratch or handed down from somewhere above. We ourselves have forged additional fetters for ourselves. We ourselves have made it a matter of daily and hourly ritual to swear our loyalty – which only loses in worth the more often it is protested . . ."

"In everything we do and say we are beset by preconceived notions and ingrained prejudices. We could do with a new Tolstoi to hit out at them by speaking the plain, unadorned truth, but instead we become more and more confirmed in them. Have you noticed how many false ideas have turned into dogma only because they are asserted in company with other ideas which are incontrovertible or sacred, so that something of the grace of indubitable and absolute truth descends on doubtful, or even utterly false propositions?"

"In our days political denunciation is not so much an activity as a whole philosophy . . ."

"The number of amoral, cruel, vicious ideas which came in under the cloak of the great word 'Revolution'!"

As I was leaving him, he again apologized very profusely for not having finished reading my play: "Or rather, I should say, I haven't even looked at it yet. I was interrupted yesterday. But no matter – we shall soon be meeting again, won't we? I like talking with you. You don't say 'yes' to everything I say, but I think you understand me."

March 11
Today's "literary Wednesday" was devoted to a discussion of writers and critics. The speakers were: Vinokur, Leonov, Derman, Pasternak, Fedin, Nusinov and Galkin. Pasternak spoke three times, but in an even more disorganized way than usual. Apart from him, Vinokur (what a clever man!) had interesting things to say.

Somebody brought *Pravda* of the 8th in which Anna Akhmatova's poem "Courage" has been printed and it was passed from hand to hand. Pasternak was radiant with joy. In *Pravda* of a few days before there was a little item saying that *Long, Long Ago* is being put on by the Red Army Theatre. Everybody congratulated me again. Pasternak invited me to come and see him next Saturday.

March 13

Ran into Pasternak this afternoon in the premises of the Writers' Union. Seeing me, he came over at once:

"Hello, Alexander Konstantinovich. You haven't forgotten you're coming to see me tomorrow?" . . .

The Union was distributing tickets for showings of the film *The German Defeat Outside Moscow*. We took a couple of tickets for Monday the 16th.

I told him that in a few days' time I was flying off to Sverdlovsk with Arbuzov. He was genuinely upset to hear it:

"I shall miss you."

We went out together. There was driving snow.

March 14

Pasternak talked to me about *Long, Long Ago* which he has now read:

"The colours of the background are brilliant and true; it is rich, authentic and mellow. The story is told with engaging artlessness. Your best quality is an entrancingly guileless imagination. The play is elegant in the proper sense of the word. Your taste never lets you down – except in one place, I should tell you straight away, where Kutuzov uses the word 'madames' . . .

There are mistakes of prosody through words being wrongly placed in the line, but this happens rarely, and it's a very minor point anyway. The songs about King Henri IV are very good, and so is the ballad of Germain. Svetlana's lullaby is exquisite – the musical quality is so intense you can almost hear the melody as you read. It is naive without being coy. In the hussars' song 'Long, Long Ago' there is a sophisticated Gypsy intonation belonging to a later period – instead of Denis Davydov you suddenly get a hint of Apukh-

91

tin here. But does it really matter, I wonder? Here, as everywhere else, you avoid stylization of the trivial kind. The comedy is made by the mice and the doll – these I find pleasing. The Frenchwoman is very good, so are Dusierre and the Spaniard – these give the true flavour of the chivalrous side of war in those days. But hasn't someone taken you to task yet because your Frenchmen aren't brutish enough? No? They will . . .

Pelymov is most interesting – this is a figure cloaked in many associations, although he's actually very sparely drawn. For some reason I hoped he would be paired off with Shura at the end, rather than with Rzhevsky. I would have made Rzhevsky into a comic figure – there is something contrived about his becoming a hero in the final scene . . . Excuse me for giving advice like this, but I can't help it, because I like the play . . . It is a youthful thing in every sense. One day people will refer to it as 'a work of the young Gladkov'. You have whetted my own desire to write a play – for which I am also grateful to you. Perhaps I will write one. But I am thinking of a drama in prose and on the subject almost of ordinary everyday existence – the other side of war* . . .

Much as I liked your play, I nevertheless feel that it does not do full justice to your capacities. When you were accepted as a member of the Union, I spoke of your unquestionable talent, of your freshness and youthful vigour, of what – if the word had not been so worn out by use – one could call your romanticism. But your most effective feature is this trusting quality of your imagination which so captivates the reader. You unfold your story confidently, never for a single second looking round anxiously in case people don't believe you . . .

It is hard for you to write a drama in verse because of the wretched condition in which our Russian prosody has come down to you. Today we need not assonance, but proper rhyme . . . In a play one should only use verse if it does not make the action sound unnatural . . . You have set out to

write verse which can be *spoken* on the stage, not *declaimed* –
something analogous to what has been done by the Arts
Theatre. If verse has any future in drama, it is only your
kind. Verse of the declamatory kind is dying out in the
theatre. There is nothing more outmoded than the plays in
verse by Gusev and others . . .

. . . Visual failures – that is, mistakes in a thing's structure –
always lead to failures of hearing, in other words, of
language . . .

You say that your new play begins with a scene in which
people dig potatoes." (I had told him the story of the play,
The Immortal One, on which I was then working with A.
Arbuzov.) "By an extraordinary coincidence, my play will
also begin in a potato field. After that it moves to an old
country estate." (I couldn't bring myself to tell him that
in our play, too, the scene later shifts to an estate!) "It is
all about cultural continuity . . . I am hoping to revive the
forgotten traditions of Ibsen and Chekhov. This is not realism
but symbolism, I suppose, isn't it?"

"Impressionism," I suggested.

"Yes, yes, quite right! . . . I have already been given an
advance by that theatre in Novosibirsk – you know, the one
where Ilovaiski plays. Do you know him?"

I replied that I had heard that he was a good actor.

"He was involved in my *Hamlet* – we have corresponded
about that and other things. I have written several letters
to him.

You remember what I told you about the air-raids on
Moscow, and how I firewatched on the roof? Well, there will
be something of that too in my play . . ."

We again discussed my idea for a biographical drama in
verse – about Petöfi. It appeals to him. He spoke about
romanticism, about Novalis, about the "Gypsy vein" in
world literature.

He is not very well, and as we talked in his room this
evening he sat lying back – for which he apologized pro-

fusely. He had no medicine and Zinaida Nikolayevna was on duty at the *Litfund* orphanage. I gave him some anti-influenza tablets I happened to have in my pocket. He asked me to look in at the orphanage on my way home, find Zinaida Nikolayevna and ask her to come home a little earlier – which I did. Z.N. listened to me in a somehow rather impassive way and said drily: "Very well. Thank you."

There is a very hard frost, and though it wasn't late when I left, the streets of Chistopol were almost empty, with only a few dim lights glowing in the windows. To get home I have to walk down Volodarski Street and Tolstoi Street – both of them very long. The whole way I felt as if borne up on wings, oblivious of the frost and the icy potholes underfoot – which are hard to negotiate even in daytime. Again and again I went over in my mind what Pasternak had said.

Can it really be? Did I really talk with him about my play? I had never hoped for anything like this even in my wildest imagination. I have not yet seen it put on the stage, but I have already received the highest accolade: his approval. Even allowing that most of it must be put down to his generosity and kindhearted indulgence, it is still more than enough to make me feel boundlessly happy.

March 17
Didn't see Pasternak in the cinema yesterday and thought he must still be sick. Tomorrow I fly to Sverdlovsk with an invitation from the Red Army Theatre in my pocket, and I decided to go and say goodbye to him. Sure enough, he was in bed. He was alone in the house and very pleased to see me. We said fond farewells. He was to have read *Romeo and Juliet* in the town theatre this evening, but has had to postpone it because of his illness. He asked me to go there and put up a notice of which he gave me the text.

I went straight to the theatre after leaving him. On the door there I found the poster announcing the reading. I took it down and am keeping it as a memento. It is written in his own hand in large letters in red and blue pencil, and is rather amusing – not to mention that it is an original manuscript by Pasternak . . .: "The few individuals who might like to hear the complete, unabridged text of *Romeo and Juliet* in my translation may do so on Tuesday March 19th at 6.00 in the evening in the building of the Town Theatre (Cultural Centre on Leo Tolstoi Street). I shall be reading it to the actors of the theatre who have kindly agreed to open their doors to all who wish to attend. In case of difficulty, please contact the actor comrade Rzhanov. B. Pasternak."

March 20
I have been in Kazan* since yesterday. I am living in the theatre, in the office of the producer, Hakkel. Yesterday Arbuzov flew from Chistopol right on my heels, and he brought with him a note to me from Pasternak, together with a typed copy of *Romeo and Juliet*:

"Dear Alexander Konstantinovich: I wish you a good journey! And as I said, I need your help: if new copies have to be made, please check them with the utmost care. Greetings to Alexei Dmitrievich [Popov]. If you need to get in touch, write to me here: c/o Vavilov, 74 Volodarski Street, Chistopol, Tartar ASSR. In Kazan the newspaper *Literature and Art* is interested in the manuscript. If you spend any length of time there, give it to them to have a look at – but in general I leave all such things to your discretion. Perhaps, if Popov is interested and takes it, you can promise to show it to them (the newspaper) later, when you pass through again on your way back from Sverdlovsk. Thank you for your kindness. Very best wishes. Yours, B. Pasternak."

There is no date on this letter, but I know that it was written on March 13, 1942. Pasternak himself had brought it, together with a package containing the manuscript, and knocked on the low window of the house where I lived – just as he had always done when inviting me out for a walk down the river.* This manuscript – or rather, type-script with handwritten corrections – was read by many people. It was typed out again in several copies by the

Distribution Department of V.U.O.A.P. [in Sverdlovsk] and I sat up a whole night checking them. Popov liked the translation, but he didn't have the people in his company to play the main parts – he kept it for a long time before turning it down, trying to devise various possible combinations of actors. I managed to interest the Maly Theatre in it and they even published an announcement in the press saying they were going to put it on, and also, I believe, signed a contract with Pasternak (at least they intended to, and I gave them his address). Vladimir Yakhontov heard about it and came to ask me for a copy. I hadn't got one handy, so he called twice again and when he eventually got it and read it, he immediately had the idea of performing the whole thing by himself. This was in the summer of 1942. I remember how we sat for a whole evening, eagerly discussing how it could be done with some cuts – and all the time glancing at our watches because of the curfew. Unfortunately, after the idea had fallen through for some reason, Yakhontov never returned the copy I had lent him.

I wrote to Pasternak about all these efforts to get his translation performed, but asked him not to write back to me for the time being since I was supposed to go off to the front with Tikhon Khrennikov as a member of a mobile troupe from the Red Army Theatre. But in the upshot our clearance by the Political Department [of the Red Army] was delayed and the troupe, headed by the producer Pildon, left without us – only to be trapped with the forces encircled near Kharkov and to perish almost to a man, except for two who escaped by chance.*

My next meeting with Pasternak was six months later, in Moscow.

3

October 22. The second autumn of the War.

For some reason the lights had been switched off in the dining-room of the Writers' Club. It was still light enough out on the street, but in the large, high-ceilinged hallway of the Club the early autumn twilight had plunged everything into a grey gloom. I heard a familiar voice, quite distinct from anyone else's: "Alexander Konstantinovich!"

Peering round I saw Pasternak sitting at a table in one corner. I went over and he jumped up and embraced me. I was overcome with embarrassment at the unexpected warmth of this welcome, but he was so straightforward and friendly that it passed immediately.

He had arrived for a few weeks from Chistopol, leaving his family there for the time being. He was delivering his new book of poems *On Early Trains* to the publishers, and had received new translating commissions. The next day he was due to read *Romeo and Juliet* at the All-Russian Theatre Association.* The next day was a hard one for me – I had to go to the militia to apply for a permit to leave for Sverdlovsk, which was rumoured to be a long and wearisome business, but I said I would try to be there.

"As usual," he then said, "I am talking only about myself and haven't asked you what you're doing – though actually I have seen a poster in the street about *Long, Long Ago*, and this told me everything. I do congratulate you most warmly. When are you going to invite me to a performance?" I replied that the production which had been running in Moscow since spring was not a success in my eyes and I preferred him not to see it. I told him of my arguments with the producer, Gorchakov, and about the primitive, crassly-obvious topical allusions interpolated into the part of Kutuzov – who was, however, despite this, brilliantly played by D. N. Orlov. In two days' time I was due to leave for Sverdlovsk, where my play had just had its première in the Red Army Theatre – a production of which I had high hopes. I had in my pocket a telegram from A. D. Popov and G. N. Boyadzhiyev telling me that it was a great success.

I realized that Pasternak now listened to what I was telling him not out of politeness alone. He was keenly interested in everything connected with the theatre. I asked him about the play he wanted to write himself. He replied that he had not finished, or for that matter, even really begun it, but that he would return to the idea.

He went on to say how pleased he was for Leonov's sake about the play he had written in Chistopol. Just during these days rumours had gone round Moscow about a phone call from Stalin to Leonov praising the play – *The Invasion* – which had recently been published. Until this phone call the attitude towards it had been wary and suspicious, but now everything changed overnight.

"I'm sure it is excellent," Pasternak remarked with his usual unstinting generosity, "the air in Chistopol is conducive to work."

I asked about his new book, and complained in passing that my copy of his previous one-volume collection of poetry was falling to bits because it had been borrowed by so many people. At this moment the lights were switched on. Somebody came over to our table and began telling us the latest news put out by the Informburo about the final German attempt to capture Stalingrad.

The next day I went to the reading of *Romeo and Juliet* at the Theatre Association. It was in the Lesser Hall and as

I was late I had to sit right at the back. In the interval I went up to Pasternak. "So you came!" he said, "Thank you! I saw you by the door and was very pleased. You bring to mind our working winter in Chistopol, and all our conversations about everything under the sun. Look – I stole this for you from the house where I stayed last night. I've written something in it, but don't read it now . . ." And he handed me his one-volume edition of 1935 in the light-blue dust-jacket. I could hardly wait to look, and I was given my chance by Professor Morozov, rosy-cheeked, expansive and voluble as ever, who came up and buttonholed Pasternak while I slipped out to the lobby and opened the book. On the reverse side of his portrait he had written in pencil in large letters:

"To Alexander Konstantinovich Gladkov. I have become very fond of you. Before my very eyes you have begun with a great success. I wish you the same good fortune in the future too. In remembrance of our winter days in Chistopol – even the hardest of them. B. Pasternak, 22/x/42, Moscow."

What greater good fortune could I have wished than to set off for the première of my play with words like these to speed me on the way!

I went back to the hall to thank Pasternak, but Professor Morozov had engaged him in conversation about certain fine points of meaning in Shakespeare's text. They were both closely hemmed in by elderly ladies of the kind who haunt such functions in the Theatre Association.

I need scarcely say that the volume was carefully packed away at the bottom of my suitcase, through which I rummaged dozens of times during the journey to get it out and read the dedication over and over again.

And as for Sverdlovsk! In Sverdlovsk I experienced the greatest joy a playwright can know: to see his first play performed uniquely well in a brilliant production. (Nine months later, when the Red Army Theatre had returned to Moscow, I again saw their production of my play in the company of Pasternak and afterwards, on a hot summer's night, walked home with him right across the city. But of this more in due course . . .)

Towards the end of the year (December 15, 1942), there was an evening meeting in the Writers' Club at which Pasternak read some of his new verse from *On Early Trains*, which was then being prepared for publication.

The general mood in those days was buoyant. The encirclement of the Germans at Stalingrad had been completed and the attempt to relieve their trapped army had failed. In North Africa the Allies had taken Tobruk and Benghazi. The French had scuttled their fleet in Toulon rather than hand it over to the enemy. The British and the Americans could not find praise great enough for the Red Army and the "Russian soul". Again – as at the same time the previous year – it was beginning to seem that victory was not far off. From January 1st, the Metro began working until 11.30 and the curfew was also now enforced only from this later hour. It was a snowy, not very cold December. The atmosphere in the Union of Writers was as "liberal" as could be, and there were optimists who thought that purges and campaigns of abuse were things of the past.

When Pasternak came out on to the low stage in the large hall (where the dining-room is now), everybody greeted him with applause. There was a large audience – almost all the Moscow writers were there, and many were in uniform, as they were passing through on their way to the front, or had come there on leave.

Pasternak was in high spirits as he read his poetry. In the discussion period afterwards he was showered with tributes and expressions of gratitude.

Wishing to confirm him in his confident, optimistic state of mind I asked for the floor and made some exuberant, romantically high-flown remarks to the effect that all the love shown for the poet this evening must be returned to us, his readers, in the guise of new, great and daring works – and I mentioned his unfinished novel, his ideas for plays and long poems. Everybody applauded once more and in his reply Pasternak said he was in duty bound to accept the summons from his readers spoken of by "Alexander Konstantinovich" – and here he smiled, showing all his white teeth, towards me where I sat next to the stage. He seemed very pleased and even rather overcome.

To give a complete picture of the general mood of unanimity, I should mention that at the end of the evening a burly, broad-shouldered young man in uniform came up and said he had very much liked what I said and agreed with every word of it. We shook hands warmly and he introduced himself: "I know you, but you don't know me: Anatoli Sofronov. I'm a poet . . ." There were many others who came up to me that evening and as I shook hands with them I was smugly convinced that my oratorical skill fully warranted their compliments. Even so, I was, of course, happiest of all for Pasternak's sake.

I believe he went back to Chistopol a few days later.

On Early Trains came out in the middle of the summer of 1943. For some reason he was always a little upset by its relatively small number of pages, saying there should have been "at least ten times more". Apart from this, he was unhappy that it combined under one cover poems dating from the mid-thirties and others written just before the war in Peredelkino. As he told me, he was conscious of a dividing line somewhere between these two cycles. He felt that a "book of poems" was always, or should be, something self-contained, reflecting a distinct phase of the poet's life. He regretted that between *Second Birth* and *On Early Trains* he had not been able to publish a volume containing what he had written up to the end of 1936.

This feeling of Pasternak's that every volume of poetry must be an entity in itself was nothing new. Nadezhda Mandelstam writes that in 1936 and 1937, when she brought him some of her husband's poems from Voronezh, Pasternak spoke to her of "the miracle of a book in the making" and looked on them not as isolated poems, but as the small component parts of a book to come, and he wrote to the exiled Mandelstam about his "book", not about his "poems".

Of Pasternak's wartime poems (a few appeared in *On Early Trains*, but most came out in his next book, *Earth's Space*), I like best of all the very first ones ("Grass Widower", "The Outpost" and "The Old Park") since they seem to follow on naturally from the pure and simple cycle of the previous ones. His attempts to depict actual scenes of war were bound to fail and the effort they cost him tells in their greater complexity and – oddly enough – in their greater similarity to the early style he had long since discarded.

I had brought with me from Chistopol a few poems which he had written out and given to me. Comparing these with the book I discovered that my hand-written copy of "The Old Park" contained four stanzas missing from the version as published.*

"The Old Park" is connected with an idea for a play in prose about the war which, as I have already mentioned, Pasternak was thinking of in 1941 and 1942. According to what he told me, the hero of the play would also have found himself lying wounded in a field hospital set up in a country house which had once belonged to his ancestors. The idea arose out of a real event: in the autumn of 1941 a military hospital was temporarily installed in an old country house in Peredelkino which had once belonged to the family of the Slavophile Samarin (it is now used by members of the Union of Writers). One of the Samarins had been a friend of Pasternak in his student days, and he had known this house already then. Did he really meet his old friend there again in the autumn of 1941, or was this simply a poetic fancy? Needless to say, a meeting of this kind would have been perfectly possible. It is easy enough to see why Pasternak omitted certain stanzas from the published version: they would have introduced too personal an element of his own life at that time, when he dreamed of isolating himself in the provinces and working on his play. "All his dreams were of the theatre . . ." could have been said then of Pasternak himself.

The first question Pasternak asked me when we met again at the very beginning of 1943 was: "Well, how are things with you in the theatre?" But before I had time to answer, he said he already knew from the posters with my name that he kept seeing, and also from a recent article in *Red Star*. (A few days earlier, in connection with the return to Moscow of the Red Army Theatre which had opened at the Subsidiary of the Arts Theatre with its production of my play, *Red Star* had run an article beginning with the words: "Why has the Soviet public taken such a liking to Alexander Gladkov's *Long, Long Ago*?" The view implied in the question seemed to me the highest of compliments – particularly as it came from the most popular and best-loved of the wartime newspapers.) He said I really must take him to see it now, and he would not accept any excuses. But as luck would have it, the actress playing the leading part, L. I. Dobrzhanskaya, was ill at that moment and performances had been cancelled. I told him this and promised to let him know when they were resumed.

We started off walking down Herzen Street together. It was a sunny day, but there were sudden showers; we were caught by one and forced to take refuge in the entrance of a house at the corner of Merzlyakov Street. We stood there for about twenty minutes. I mentioned his *On Early Trains*, which had just come out, but he seemed reluctant to talk about it and replied in rather embarrassed fashion that the book was "wretchedly short", and that the disparity between the different parts of it was not at all to his liking. From this he went on to speak with great feeling about the "inadequacy" of his literary existence and recalled the words in my speech at his reading that winter about what he "owed" his readers. He had now brought with him to Moscow his completed translation of *Antony and Cleopatra* but, though he felt it had come out well, it gave him little pleasure because "at a time like this one should not make do with translations". He no longer seemed so cheerful and confident as he had been six months before. I felt he was again prey to the dissatisfaction with himself that I had seen so often in him. In the brief outline he gave me of his plans, the theatre once more bulked largest of all.

I told him that in the spring I had been to see Vladimir Ivanovich Nemirovich-Danchenko, not very long before his death, and he had told me that he was waiting impatiently for Pasternak to finish his *Antony and Cleopatra* – "my favourite play", as he said. He had already sketched out a plan for the production. "But without Vladimir Ivanovich", Pasternak replied, "it won't be put on. You see what bad luck I have with the theatre. Everything may seem to be going well, but then there is always a snag of some kind . . ." – and he recalled sadly how the Arts Theatre had suddenly ceased rehearsals of *Hamlet*. Already at that time there were vague stories going around that this had happened because of Stalin's personal intervention. It was not that he had directly ordered them not to put it on – he had simply expressed his surprise at the idea of the Arts Theatre doing it. This of course was enough for it to be taken out of rehearsal at once. Stalin was probably against it for the same reason that he was against putting on *Macbeth* or *Boris Godunov*: such portraits of rulers whose road to power had been strewn with corpses did not appeal to him in the least.

I now learned from Pasternak that this time he had brought his family back with him from Chistopol, but after the hard winter his apartment was not habitable, and for the moment they had no place of their own to live in: "For the time being we're staying with the Asmuses, but I go over to my brother's place to work." He gave me the telephone numbers of both apartments and asked me to ring him as soon as I knew when my play would be performed again.

This conversation between us was at the very beginning of July, before the battle of the Kursk "bulge" had begun. It was rainy in Moscow during that summer of 1943, particularly in the first half. The continuing lull on the battle fronts was beginning to seem ominous. At the Moscow première of *Long, Long Ago* I had been present at a conversation between the producer, A. D. Popov, and A. S. Shcherbakov, who had come specially for the occasion. When Popov, commenting on the theatre's return to Moscow, said something to the effect that "the worst is now behind us", Shcherbakov looked dubious and said, "I am not sure you haven't come back too soon." The end of June and beginning of July were heavy with foreboding. The mysterious inactivity of the Germans and our own feeling of uncertainty were disturbing. Judging by the remark that Shcherbakov had let slip – he was head of the "Political Directorate" and a confidant of Stalin's – this mood was a general one, shared even by the men at the top.

Quite recently I was able to read some letters written by Pasternak at this period. Here is something he said less than a month before his return from Chistopol to Moscow: "Through the younger generation and the theatre, I should like to establish a proper relationship with destiny, reality, and the war. I am coming back to fight for my true self and my allotted part in life, because my present existence is unimaginably piteous . . ." The letter is dated June 10, 1942. This is very similar to what he said to me in our conversation, though with me the tone was rather different – a little more hopeful, I would say. At this time he looked on me as someone favoured by fortune who had seized the fire-bird by the tail. It may be that he was infected by my own happy mood or at least, with his natural tact, did not want to spoil it by introducing a jarring note.

When I next saw Pasternak, the battle of the Kursk bulge had already got under way – it was being fought with enormous ferocity and the outcome was still in doubt. We met at the Theatre Association, where he gave a reading of *Antony and Cleopatra*.

The small room was packed tight with people – mostly the usual ladies who frequented the Association and also young students from the Institute of Drama. The long summer evening was only beginning and it was still completely light outside in the streets, but in the Lesser Hall on the top floor (where he had also read *Romeo and Juliet*) it was dark because of the drawn blinds. The place was lit by lamps.

I noticed something I had evidently not seen at our previous meeting, namely that Pasternak had gone very much greyer since the winter. He read with glasses, but took them off whenever he looked up from his manuscript. On this occasion he almost entirely dispensed with his usual long-drawn-out introductory remarks, simply describing the play as "the story of a love affair between a libertine and a seductress" and saying that, in his opinion, it was the most "objective and realist" of Shakespeare's tragedies, and thus inevitably reminiscent of *Anna Karenina* or *Madame Bovary*. He read with marked enthusiasm and very effectively. The translation is excellent, even better than *Romeo and Juliet* – a magnificent, full-bodied rendering of the original and done with a most delicate sense of all its beauty. At the end of the scene where Enobarbus tells the story of Cleopatra and her love for Antony, the audience broke into spontaneous applause. Pasternak smiled with pleasure, took off his glasses, gave a rather awkward little bow and said: "Just wait – it gets even better . . ." Everybody laughed, including Pasternak himself. He put on his glasses again and continued.

In the prose passages, he rather naively attempted to put some "expression" into his voice and read "like an actor" – he was, of course, not very successful. It would even, perhaps, have been a little ludicrous if it had not been for his unaffected charm. In the tragic scenes he became touchingly worked up and read superbly.

It was getting stuffy in the hall. There had just been a thunderstorm, but it was impossible to open the windows. An interval was announced.

I made my way over to Pasternak. He said he had not noticed me, though he had "looked around as usual" for me, and again quite unexpectedly began to speak about my words at his reading that winter, and about his failure to "live up to expectations" – here he was, "again coming to Moscow with a piece of work which is not original". I praised the translation. He smiled gratefully, and asked whether Dobrzhanskaya had recovered yet: "Don't forget to ring me when the play is put on." Nearby Kruchenykh was hovering with his inseparable briefcase, from which he took a pen and ink-well, asking both of us to write something in an exercise-book.

The reading now continued. In the banquet scene on Pompey's galley, Pasternak was suddenly himself the first to laugh at the words "'Tis a strange serpent", and everybody else laughed with him. We all listened with bated breath to the part about Cleopatra's death and the closing scenes. When he finished there was wild applause. Everybody got to their feet and went on clapping. Pasternak took off his glasses, bowing and smiling. The ovation still went on. Kruchenykh climbed on a chair and started shouting something. I braced myself for an embarrassing scene, but everything passed off fairly harmlessly when Kruchenykh offered an impromptu tribute:

"This Shakespeare would not have dreamed of
– that Cleopatra should pass before us in your carriage . . ."

There was renewed applause and Kruchenykh beamed. Pasternak looked bashful and smiled indulgently. He was already surrounded by a crowd of ladies.

I went out on the street feeling purified by these electric discharges of true art. The air after the storm was fresh and the greenery on the boulevard indescribable. I didn't feel like going home and sat for a long time on a bench near the Pushkin statue. Somewhere in the distance I could hear songs from *Long, Long Ago* coming over a loudspeaker – they had already become popular. It occurred to me that perhaps Pasternak might also be listening to them at this very moment as he walked home.

At last Dobrzhanskaya recovered and the performances of my play were renewed. But by now I was doubtful about ringing Pasternak. Perhaps he had just asked to be invited out of his usual kindheartedness? I was still hesitating and brooding on it, when I suddenly ran into him in the Writers' Club.

It had been raining all day, but he was wearing light-coloured cotton trousers and white canvas shoes which were now splattered with mud and soaked through. He asked why I hadn't phoned him – he had seen an advertisement about my play in the newspapers. We made a date for the following Saturday which would be the day after next, July 31st. I was to bring him tickets that morning, at his brother's apartment. I wrote down the address – it turned out to be in the same street as mine, the former Bolshoi Znamenski Street, now renamed Gritsevets Street, after an airman who had been killed in the war.

The rain continued to pour down, so we stood for a while in the entrance, waiting for it to slacken off, and talked about the latest news – the victorious Soviet offensive at Orel, the fall and arrest of Mussolini, and the demonstrations in Milan. I told him about the remarkable and unexpected reaction to the American film *Mission to Moscow** being shown in the city. Full of political naivety, it was being greeted with laughter by the audience and this Hollywood attempt to give serious dramatic treatment to the events of our times was thus having the effect of a hilarious comedy.

At eleven in the morning of July 31st, I duly set out for the Pasternak apartment with two tickets and a copy of *On Early Trains* which I wanted him to sign for me.

I had often been past this strange half-glass building in the Corbusier style which abuts on the street at a sharp angle and has another side facing Gogol Boulevard. I had noted the number of the apartment wrongly and found it with some difficulty. The building was not quite as imposing inside as outside: the plaster on the walls of the staircase was crumbling and there was a depressing smell of cats. The windows were all boarded up with plywood. I stumbled against a bucket full of sand. The bell did not work, so I knocked. The door was opened by Pasternak himself. He took me into a small, rather narrow room which looked out onto the boulevard. This was where his brother, an architect, lived.

There was a pile of old books on the desk and Pasternak told me that, at the suggestion of Chagin, he was compiling a small volume of his selected works. It was to contain – as he put it – all his "most descriptive" things. His *Romeo and Juliet* was about to appear, and he was now being invited to translate *Othello* (and *Macbeth* also, I think): "But I am not certain I'll take it on. It's time to give up translating – when all is said and done, it is only a substitute for real work. What you said that time at my reading was quite right." Involuntarily imitating his manner, I replied that it had been far from my mind to give him a weapon against himself in his moments of dissatisfaction with himself, that my words had been intended not as a reproach but only as the expression of a hope, etc. . . . "Yes, that is exactly it, and you were quite right. You said more than you intended, and I am grateful to you for it . . ."

I asked him to try not to be late and left the tickets and the book with him (he promised to return the book to me at the theatre) and went home to count the minutes until the evening.

And at last the evening came – though it was still very early for summertime, since theatre performances began now at half past six. By six I was already standing at the entrance to the grounds of the Central Red Army Club where the Red Army Theatre played in the summer. It had started to rain several times during the day, but every time the sun came out again and the sky was now completely clear. It was almost hot.

Pasternak arrived at twenty past six. He was alone. I no longer remember who was supposed to come with him and what had prevented the other person. He returned the second ticket to me and I was inwardly very pleased – it meant I would be able to sit next to him and talk with him during all three intermissions.

I have already mentioned Pasternak's astonishing spontaneity, his childlike enthusiasm as a spectator at the theatre. Anybody who saw the Red Army performance of *Long, Long Ago* with the original cast (Dobrzhanskaya, Pestovski, Konovalov, Khokhlov, Khomiakov, Ratomski, Shakhet, Khodurski) will remember how it "went over" with the audience, and on that particular evening the most naively enthusiastic member of it was certainly Pasternak. He laughed loudly, shouted "marvellous", "magnificent", and joined in all the bursts of applause which frequently broke out in the middle of an act. He watched with total absorption and the closest possible attention, not however forgetting the nervous author at his side, often turning to me as though inviting me to share his delight.

In the first intermission he took *On Early Trains* from his pocket and gave it to me. When I had a moment, I looked inside. On the back of the title-page he had written in large letters which took up the entire space:

"To dear Alexander Konstantinovich Gladkov, whose early and rapid success is near and precious to me. B. Pasternak, 31/vii/43."

I was too worked up that evening to remember the details of what Pasternak and I talked about in the intermissions and on the way home. Nor could I make any notes later that night – by the time I got home I was literally numb with fatigue, since apart from everything else, we walked the whole way home on foot, from Commune Square to Kropotkin Square. I made a few notes only the next day.

I had not doubted that he would like the play. By this time its success was evident for all to see – to the point of being quite out of my hands already and of outgrowing me, as it were, in a way that sometimes seemed frightening. If even some of our glum, strait-laced Party functionaries were beginning to smile happily and unselfconsciously, if the ushers stood in the aisles watching it for the umpteenth time, if people started coming up as far away from the theatre as the corner of Durov Street to ask if you had a spare ticket to sell – then I had no cause for anxiety about the ever-trusting and grateful Pasternak who was so well-disposed towards me in any case. I was agitated not because I had any doubts, but thanks to a sense of fulfilment which was extraordinarily complete and unqualified. I am not writing about myself, but about Pasternak, so will not dwell on it further – but I think people may believe me if I say that this was one of the very happiest evenings in my life.

At the end of the play Pasternak took back my copy of *On Early Trains* and wrote something else on the inside of the cover:

"To Gladkov from a witness of his triumph, with joy and love . . ."

And now we were walking home at night through the streets of wartime Moscow – Tsvetnoi Boulevard, Neglinnaya, Sverdlov Square, Mokhovaya. The blackout was no longer total: in the main thoroughfares there were gleaming rows of street-lamps switched on to one fifth of their power. Tramcars were dimly lit and sometimes cars pierced the dark-blue July night with their headlights. The bizarre silhouettes of anti-aircraft balloons could be seen swaying slightly in the air high up above – they were always sent up, it so happened, just around the time the theatres ended. In the daytime their silvery carcasses gave them the appearance of huge mythological beasts peacefully grazing on the grass of the city's public gardens, but now, in the air, they looked mysterious and menacing.

It was Pasternak who suggested going home on foot. He talked while I listened:

"You're a very fortunate person, and you don't even realize it." (I did not demur, though I believe I *had* realized it that evening!) "You are a very fortunate person, and today I envy you . . . I may be mistaken, but I had the impression that your play has almost no empty spaces – no unfilled areas between the idea and its realization. Even earlier

I could see what a good play it is, but I only appreciated it to the full this evening. I seem to remember making one or two carping remarks. There is no more point in them now than there would be in worrying about an ink-blot on your plan of campaign after the winning of a battle . . . I am always dreaming of a success on the stage myself and I imagine something just like what happened tonight – the total capture of the audience, the sound of its sighing contentedly or catching its breath. The worst story-tellers are those who worry that people may not believe them. You tell your story on the stage confidently and boldly, and belief in you is total. You once worked with Meyerhold – did you learn this from him, or is it something inborn? . . . Even if you had not told me already how you wrote the play, I should have guessed that you wrote it quickly. Things as felicitous as this are always written quickly. I have always felt that the success of anything is invariably contained in the very first notion of it. That's how it was with you, wasn't it?" (At this point I confessed that I now dreamed of going on to write prose.) "No, no – write for the theatre. This is a very rare kind of gift and I would give a great deal to possess it myself . . ."

We talked about plays written by poets and I told him about Marina Tsvetayeva's supercilious preface to her remarkable drama *The End of Casanova*, where she draws a sharp distinction between poetry and the theatre and states that she does not herself like the theatre and is not drawn to it. Pasternak had not read this play and was unaware of what she says in the preface:

"She may have said this, yet even so she wrote several plays – and you yourself say this is an excellent one. Marina was a woman and sometimes said things only because she wanted to hear them immediately contradicted . . ."

He expressed great admiration for Blok's idea of writing a play on the theme, as he put it, of Russia's renascence in the factory age. On the other hand, he thought Blok's plan for a play about Christ was the "milk and water blasphemy of an intellectual", explaining that he would have been able to take it if there had been more blood and passion, even in a spirit of denial . . .

He talked again about his work on Shakespeare:

"I am tired of translating, and am probably unfair about what I have gained from it. In the material sense, it has quite simply been my salvation. And one day, perhaps, I shall understand what I have learned from this Titan. The most amazing thing about him is that, as a poet, he had an inner freedom quite beyond our ken, even though it was bound up with a multitude of prejudices and superstitious beliefs. He believed in witches, yet valued this freedom of his above all else. We do not believe in witches and can study the minutest cell under a microscope, but we are not free in any respect . . ."

"It is only untruth that beats about the bush. Truth has need of few words. The shortest words are 'yes' and 'no'. I should like to write a play of which the tone would be just as natural as with people who always reply 'yes' or 'no', never 'well, you see . . .' or 'now, it's like this . . .'"

We returned to the subject of the war – something it was impossible not to talk about in those days . . . I thought Pasternak was in a much more serene state of mind than in the first days after his return from Chistopol – I remember no other time during the whole of the war when there were so many bright hopes for the future and such feverish antici-pation of victory as at the end of the summer of 1943. After beating back the German offensive at Kursk, the Red Army was now advancing towards Orel. The Allies were masters of Sicily and the Mussolini régime had fallen. There was a general mood of confidence and exultation which inevitably affected Pasternak as well. His usual sense of acute dissatisfaction with himself now found an outlet in an exaggerated feeling that what he was doing was too little when set by the side of the enormous exertions of the country as a whole. I was left with an impression of his deep sincerity when he spoke of his duty, as a poet, to our life and times.

His personal strategy was to try to get one or more of his Shakespeare translations produced on the stage, thereby establishing direct contact with the theatre, and then to write a play of his own. After that he wanted to write a long poem in realistic vein (he spoke of it as "a novel in verse") about the war and wartime life – he had already written parts of the first chapter, telling the story of a front-line soldier's homecoming and a few other episodes. Several fragments from it appeared under the title "Nightglow"* in the 1961 volume of Pasternak's poems. I still have a copy of the beginning of this poem given to me by Pasternak (though I am not sure when exactly – in 1943, or later). I remember how he once described it as being in the style of Nekrasov – evidently on account of the richness of detail about everyday life, the colloquial manner and the narrative framework. When I happened to ask Pasternak some time just after the end of the war what had become of this poem, he told me he had been advised against carrying on with it by Fadeyev, who was "horrified" by his realistic description of all the anomalies and difficulties of life during the war. At about the same time Fadeyev had been advising Soviet writers to model themselves on Turgenev rather than on Chekhov.* The connection here is clear enough.

One does not need the intuition of a Cuvier to be able to reconstruct from the existing fragments what the whole work would have been like. The poem contained an open polemic against the bogus literature of the Stalin years, and Pasternak made no bones about it: "Self-advancement was not sought / by the writer of an earlier day. / . . . By not embellishing his every thought, / now, too, he could become a Priestley or a Hemingway."

No wonder that Fadeyev was "horrified" and that, having devoted his entire life and not inconsiderable talent to the wholehearted service of the Stalin cult, he should have persuaded Pasternak to abandon work on his poem. This was one of those compromises with his own literary integrity that Pasternak felt ashamed of in later years. I have talked about "Nightglow" at some length because there are many who find it hard to understand how Boris Pasternak, the "pure" lyric poet and incomparable observer of nature, could have written the works of his final years. Unaware of his previous attempts to talk openly and frankly about what was going on in the world around him, some people have even alleged that he must earlier have led a "double life". This is certainly not the case. The story of his unfinished narrative poem is proof enough. The fact is, in other words, that during the war years, apart from translating Shakespeare and occasionally writing lyric verse of his own, he was also working on both a play and a long poem on topical themes. He lived in those days not in an "ivory tower", but in the same kind of cramped, unheated lodgings as everybody else. Furthermore, I never noticed in him any tendency to be snobbishly exclusive in literary matters. Once he said to me: "I am reading Simonov. I want to understand the nature of his success." Another time I heard him speak with great enthusiasm about the first chapters of Tvardovski's *Vasili Terkin*. He liked Vasili Grossman's *The People is Immortal*. In August 1943 he visited the front together with A. Serafimovich and R. Ostrovskaya. If he avoided reading the newspapers, it was not because he wanted to cut himself off from the events of the day, but because he could not stand the cloying rhetoric in which they were served up. In those war years I do not remember a single meeting with him during which we failed to talk about the latest news from the front line and from the rest of the world.

In my notes on our conversation after the theatre on the night of July 31, 1943, I recorded in detail – with the natural egocentricity of a young man – almost everything he said to me about my play and put down the rest only in the form of headings, such as "Spoke about his long poem", and in writing about it here, I am simply reconstructing the gist of his words at the time. It is hard for me to say when exactly he gave up his work on it. I believe it was either at the end of 1943 or the beginning of 1944. But at the time of our conversation he still thought of it – together with his play in prose about the war – as one of the major works he had in hand, and he was longing to get his translations out of the way in order to concentrate only on these.

Describing at this distance in time that memorable July night I cannot help wondering whether I was not so intoxicated by my own success and Pasternak's praise that I am imputing to him my own state of mind – which was one of almost childlike gleefulness. But I think not. If there had been any discrepancy between his mood and mine, I would almost certainly have sensed it and remarked on it in my notes. I already knew Pasternak pretty well by then and I could sometimes tell what frame of mind he was in even before he began to speak. As I remember him that night he was in very high spirits and full of friendly concern. The very fact of his suggesting we go home on foot showed what a good mood he was in. We strode along all the way to Kropotkin Square, which was quite a distance. He was going to spend the night in his brother's apartment and I saw him to the door. "Do you remember our walks along the Kama?" he asked, as we said goodbye, "I am sometimes nostalgic for them . . . Thank you for the evening! I wish you every success in the future as well."

He went into the dark hallway and as I left him, I felt sorry I had less than a block to go. I just wanted to go on walking, talking about something or reciting poetry. But as soon as I got home, I immediately fell fast asleep, without even touching my diary.

Whenever Pasternak took a fancy to anything he was extraordinarily generous, lavishing praise with princely open-handedness. I scarcely ever remember him making a negative comment – either he praised or said nothing at all. Strange as it may seem, he was always least inclined to speak up in favour of anything which he thought had been done under his influence, or showed some affinity to him and, conversely, he was very often most enthusiastic about work that was far from his own or even at the opposite pole. I well remember his glowing words about Tvardovski's *Vasili Terkin*, which he described as a "miracle of total assimilation to popular speech".

Once, at a literary evening, he was supposed to take the floor after Pavel Vasilyev, who recited his famous "To Natalie". Pasternak was so enchanted by it that he went up on the stage and announced to the audience that he thought it would be out of place and churlish of him to read anything after this "brilliant poem". On another occasion (while we were still in Chistopol) he talked to me about the extraordinarily rapid growth of the young Vasilyev as a poet and said that after his death he had never encountered such an exuberant imagination in anyone else. As I had known Vasilyev personally and seen a different side to his poetry, I begged to differ, but Pasternak insisted on his highly-flattering opinion.

He was almost as complimentary about Vasilyev's verse when he was asked to give his view in connection with the poet's posthumous rehabilitation in 1956. I believe Pasternak was even somehow drawn to everything remote from his own individual approach and that he set particular value on it, or – as he had no hesitation in saying himself – "felt envious" of it. Needless to say, this was a very special kind of envy on a high literary level which would be better described as a hankering after ways to broaden his own scope.

I have been able to read Pasternak's letters to Mandelstam. They are very interesting in this respect, as a few quotations will show. In a letter written in 1924, Pasternak said: "I shall never in my life be able to write anything comparable to *Stone*.* And how long ago it was done, and how many Americas were discovered in it, quietly and without fanfares – Americas that people later rediscovered more picturesquely only because they spent such a long time wandering around as they neared their journey's end, floundering in the

Saragossa seas at its approaches, thrashing about and regaling us with their aquatic feats – all guaranteed to thrill, like steam engines or policemen on the cinema screen." In the same letter he asks Mandelstam: "What good do you see in me?" . . . In another letter written in 1928 after the publication of Mandelstam's *Selected Works*, he wrote: "Its perfection and fullbodiedness are astonishing, and these lines of mine can be no more than a cry of delight and awe . . ."

He spoke with similar enthusiasm in another letter about Mandelstam's *The Noise of Time* and went on to ask: "Why don't you write a major novel? You already have it in you – all you need do is write it." At the beginning of 1937, after reading the manuscript of *Voronezh Notebooks*, Pasternak wrote to Mandelstam in his place of exile: "Your new book is remarkable . . . I am terribly pleased on your behalf. I envy you. In the most felicitous things (and there are many) the inner melody is expressed in the vocabulary, in the metaphors, in a rare purity and distinctiveness . . ."

Pasternak's capacity to be delighted and astonished as he felt himself sharing the creative experience of other poets of a quite different kind, the exceptional absence of any narrowness in his perception of their work, was combined in a curious and engaging way with a tendency to pass excessively harsh judgement on what he had done himself. I have already mentioned what he told me about his feelings of being a "Khlestakov", about all his work until the end of the thirties being weak and not on the mark. I have heard it suggested that this streak of self-deprecation appeared only as he was approaching old age and going through an inner crisis. This is not so. In one of his letters written to Mandelstam in the mid-twenties there is a passage where he says: "I have just been correcting a typewritten copy of *Spektorski* and have given myself a pledge to ignore the truth. It is boring and insipid, but I shall just take myself firmly in hand . . ."

In one of our very last conversations during a chance meeting at Peredelkino (of which I shall say more later), not long after he had finished *Doctor Zhivago* and it was due to come out in Italy, Pasternak said with anguish that he fully expected the effect of the novel would be to make foreign publishers feel they must "drag out of oblivion and translate all the babblings and scribblings of those years when I still did not know how to write, think or speak – and was even doing my best not to learn . . ." When he talked in this vein, he was referring not only to *A Twin in the Clouds*, but also to *My Sister Life, Above the Barriers,** the long poems on the revolution of 1905, and almost everything else. Speaking of the long poems, he complained how "empty and prolix" they were. Listening to him uttering such views of himself – I had first heard them in Chistopol – I was appalled and dismayed, and it was only after I got to know him well and became used to him that I was able to relate them to the basic feature of his character: his extraordinary modesty and his insistence on making the highest demands of himself. G. O. Vinokur, one of the most intelligent men I have ever met, who knew Pasternak well and liked him, once said, when we happened to talk about this side of Pasternak's character, that his modesty was bound up with a rare sense of his own worth. "I am never sure where modesty ends and supreme self-esteem begins," Vinokur said with a smile. It may be so, but it is no easy thing to understand a person as complex as Pasternak.

In the late autumn or early winter of 1943, the Writers' Club arranged an unusual poetry evening at which famous poets were invited to read their early verse. Among those who did so, I remember, were Kamenski, Sergei Gorodetski, Antokolski, Aseyev, Dmitri Petrovski, Ehrenburg and also, I believe, Tikhonov. Most of them read with a supercilious smile of condescension towards their early efforts, sometimes almost to the point of making fun of them. Only Ehrenburg read the poems written in his youth – a far cry from those of later years – with an air of respect for his past which the audience found captivating. When Pasternak's turn came and his name was called out by the person presiding he at first refused to read anything at all, but when people clapped and shouted "Please!", he said that in that case he would read his latest poems, because his early ones were of no interest to him. And he recited several of his poems on the war, and an extract from the narrative one I have described earlier.

Before this, at the beginning of October (7th), I happened to meet him on the Polyanka.* He was wearing a shabby mackintosh, an outlandish broad-brimmed hat and had a rucksack over his shoulder. He asked about my play and said he would like to see it again (I interpreted this as a polite gesture and decided not to take it up with him later on the phone – I was so afraid of seeming to impose myself that perhaps he may sometimes have thought me rather offhanded). He said he had not yet got a place to live and was "still a burden on the Asmuses". When I asked him what he was doing at the moment, he said he was at last about to get down to writing something of his own. As we were saying goodbye, completely changing the subject, he suddenly said: "We really did have a good time in Chistopol – as I realize if only from the fact that it is always so pleasant to see you . . ." He also told me during this meeting that an excerpt from his narrative poem would shortly be appearing in *Pravda.**

On November 3 we met at a rehearsal of Shostakovich's 8th Symphony in the Great Hall of the Conservatory. My seat happened to be right behind his. Before the concert began, Khrennikov had told me that our troops had entered Kiev. Pasternak was already in his seat when I came into the hall, and I leaned over to greet him and tell him the good news. I have a very clear recollection of his joyful reception of it. At that time we all lived in expectation of news from the front line and Pasternak was no exception. (Actually, this particular piece of news turned out to be premature – the official communiqué on the capture of Kiev was put out only on the day before the Anniversary of the Revolution, on November 6.)

In 1943-4 poems by Pasternak appeared quite frequently in the newspapers. Apart from the item in *Pravda* mentioned above, *Red Star* printed "The Death of a Sapper", "Pursuit", "On Reconnaissance", "Boundlessness" and *Literature and Art* had "Winter Begins", and others.* The translation of *Romeo and Juliet* was published, and *Earth's Space*, as well as another, small volume of his selected poems,* were in preparation (they actually appeared only in 1945).

My brother, who was in one of the Kolyma* camps, wrote to me that he had been given a precious gift there. One of his fellow prisoners, the poet and critic Igor Postupalski, had presented him on his birthday with a tattered volume of Pasternak's verse. I could not refrain from telling this to Pasternak. It had a great effect on him. He began to question me about my brother and what had happened to him. We were talking in a tramcar and people were listening, so I felt it hard to speak freely. But Pasternak, without lowering his voice, kept asking more and more questions. "Thank you for telling me," he said at last, "this is very important to me. I am grateful to him for writing about it. I am grateful to them all for remembering me . . ." He was in an emotional state and often harked back to this conversation later on, always asking me about my brother every time we met.

At the end of August 1944, on my return from a visit to the 2nd Ukrainian army group which was already on Rumanian territory, I met Pasternak at lunch in the restaurant of the Writers' Club. He asked for my impressions and said scarcely anything about himself. All I learned, in answer to a direct question, was that he had given up work on the narrative poem and was finishing his translation of *Othello*. I asked whether he was going to translate the whole of Shakespeare and he answered my question with a joke. When I enquired about his play, he just shrugged.

On November 11, we met again on Piatnitskaya Street. I was just on my way from the building in Lavrushinski Street, and he was on his way there. I turned round and walked back with him, and we stood talking at the entrance for another twenty minutes. He had by now completed *Othello* and again swore to me he would take on no more translations. Again I asked him about the long poem. It was now that he told me how he had read it to Fadeyev who had advised him to abandon it. He was silent for a moment, then he said with a grin that he had two books about to come out and it would be a pity to jeopardize them at this point. So far no book of his had been pulped on higher orders – this was something he was to experience only in the future. We talked about various recent events: the re-election of Roosevelt for a fourth term, the battles near Budapest, the replacement of Sudakov by Prov Sadovski at the Maly Theatre after a devastating article in *Pravda* ("That's just my luck again," commented Pasternak – "Sudakov was hoping to produce *Romeo and Juliet* in the spring"), the putting on of Alexei Tolstoi's *Ivan the Terrible*, Shklovski's book *Encounters* which had been mutilated by pernickety editors and censors – lengthy sections on Zoshchenko, Shostakovich and the inventor Kostikov (apparently because of some sordid affair involving him) were left out, Dzhambul did not appear under his real name, and in general the whole thing had been reduced to a shambles. We next discussed the rumour about our entry into the war against Japan. I had never before known him to be less "withdrawn" from the world around him than on this occasion, and I even commented jokingly on it, saying that he was not living up to his reputation as a man with his head in the clouds. He smiled wanly.

At the beginning of February *Earth's Space* came out. There was little new in it – the same poems as in *On Early Trains* with the addition of a few wartime ones. Once again the censors had taken out "Waltz with Ghosts"* describing a Christmas party through the eyes of a child – probably because of the word "ghost".† The book was printed on

---

† This poem was published only in the volume that came out in 1961.

very bad paper and Pasternak said to me once that it inspired him with "physical revulsion".

In 1945 and 1946 I saw only little of him. The war was over, but the first post-war years were difficult ones – not only in a material sense, but even more because there was no longer anything to look forward to, in the way that we had looked forward to victory. Stavski, after at last falling into disfavour with Stalin, had been killed at the front, but there were plenty of other "Skalozubs" besides him. The "cult of personality" became increasingly blatant and hideous. Akhmatova and Zoshchenko were expelled from the Union of Writers. The dead weight of Stalin's lawless tyranny pressed down on us ever more heavily. Even the "safe" and complaisant Fedin was blasted for the second part of his memoir on Gorki.

At this period Pasternak spent most of his time in Peredel-kino, which I visited only rarely. We thus no longer ran into each other by chance, and I made no attempt to seek him out – my own morale at this time was pretty low. A comedy written by me had been removed from the theatre repertoires together with other blacklisted plays. In my previous conversations with Pasternak I had always somehow been the one to strike a note of incurable optimism, but now it would have sounded both ludicrous and false. On the other hand, I still could not stomach people who did nothing but moan and sow panic – it seemed inconceivable that everything would not soon be cleared up in some way and a normal state of affairs restored. Reason found it hard to accept that such an arbitrary method of rule could settle down as a system. As in previous years, every manifestation of it was still seen as a misunderstanding or as a ghastly accident of some kind. In other words, we looked for logic in unreason and tried to find justification for the unjustifiable. Pasternak had always regarded me as someone permanently favoured by fortune and I did not want him to see me in my depressed state, with all my confidence gone.

But in various ways I got indirect news about him and his mood. Once, the unfailingly cheerful Professor Morozov† gleefully read out to me an impromptu epigram composed by Pasternak: "Hand in hand with Morozov and Virgil, I descend to Inferno's lowest circle / They make it look like sheer perfection / and I have no doubt of the Resurrection." The bitterness of the irony is evident enough. On another occasion Kruchenykh showed me a birthday message in verse which he had received from Pasternak.* It included the following lines:

> I'm fast becoming old and grey,
> But you grow more robust by the day.
> O God, how alien I find
> This put-on joie de vivre of ours;
> But I'm the guiltier one –
> You're not to be reproached.
> Like me, you have been spared by fate
> Only in that it hasn't spoiled you . . .
> Let us institute an order
> For those whose ways are just
> – Although they live on bread and water!

This poem was written at the end of February 1946. Its slightly bantering tone does not altogether disguise the very serious heartsearchings to which the poet returned several times later on (in his poem "Fame's not a pretty sight",* and in *An Essay in Autobiography*).

These two years, 1945 and 1946, will probably be seen by Pasternak's future biographers as the period in which he underwent a profound inner change. Although it can only be a matter for speculation, we may surmise that what happened was this: his acute and painful sense of having reached a dead end in his work (the abandonment of the narrative poem and failure to do anything for the theatre)

† Mikhail Morozov: well-known Shakespeare scholar and admirer of Pasternak's translations, on which he wrote articles and commentaries.

had brought on such an extreme state of dissatisfaction with himself that he decided, as the only possible solution, to return to the novel begun a long time before and then put aside, and whose significance for his literary career he greatly exaggerated and which, after he had completed it, he was to regard as the only work he need not be ashamed of. In a letter of this period to someone whose correspondence with him I have quoted before, he wrote: "I have only been writing a little of my own, but now I am going to work more on my prose novel which will deal with the whole of our life from the beginning, not so much in its literary as in its substantive aspect . . ." And further on: "My relations with certain people at the front, at poetry readings, in one or two remote corners, and particularly in the West have proved to be more numerous, straightforward and simple than I could ever have imagined in my wildest dreams.* This has had the unique and magic effect of simplifying and making easier my inner life, my thoughts and my work – while at the same time and in equal measure complicating my outward existence. The latter is difficult – particularly since my previous forbearance and amiability have vanished without trace. Not only do Tikhonov and his like as well as most other members of the Union of Writers no longer exist for me, not only do I deny them, but I also lose no opportunity of saying so openly and plainly. And they, of course, are quite right to pay me back in kind. It goes without saying that our forces are unequally matched, but the die is cast as far as I am concerned, and I have no choice . . ." This letter is not dated, but in it Pasternak refers to the death of his father, the well-known painter Leonid Pasternak, who died in the middle of 1945 – which means that the letter was probably written some time in the second half of the same year.

It is not always necessary to seek direct connections between a poet's verse and actual moments in his life, but sometimes they are self-evident. This passage in Pasternak's letter reads like a prose version of the famous lines in his "Hamlet" poem written at about the same time: "Yet the order of the acts is planned / And the end of the way inescapable . . ." I myself heard from him that he had returned to work on the novel when we happened to meet by chance on the Mohkovaya,* near the Metro station, in the last hours of December 31, 1945. I asked him whether it was the same work of which he had published several extracts in *Literary Gazette** already in the mid-thirties, under the title "From a novel about 1905". He replied that something of this would go into the novel, but that the basic concept had been very much changed. And then he added a strange remark which I noted down word for word at the time: "I am writing this novel about people who could have been representatives of my school – if I had one . . ." Having said this, he smiled and looked slightly sheepish in a way that was somehow all his own. A light powdering of snow had settled on his collar and cap. It suited him very well. I reminded him that at this time four years previously I had come to call on him in Chistopol, and he had been laid up with lumbago and had read Victor Hugo on Shakespeare to me. "Was that four years ago?" "Does it seem a lot or a little to you?" I asked. "Both a lot and a little – a lot to have lived through, but not much work to show for it."

The New Year crowds were surging all around us. He seemed in no particular hurry, but we were standing in people's way and being jostled. We either had to move on or say goodbye. We wished each other all the very best and went off on our separate ways. After a few paces I looked back and saw him walking slowly towards the Volkhonka* under the light New Year's snow . . .

Extracts from another letter, dated November 26, 1946, to the same person as before:

"I now have a chance of working on something without being forced to think of how to earn my daily bread. I want to write about the whole of our life, from Blok to the war that has just finished – if possible in 10 or 12 chapters, no more. You can imagine what a hurry I am in to work, how much I fear that something might happen to prevent me finishing it, and how often I have to break off as it is . . . At present, quite independently of my own volition, things of very great meaning are entering into the orbit of my destiny . . . I have always known that to strike a true moral or aristocratic note more is required than one's own experience of life, and that one must take a much wider circle into one's purview . . . I can now no longer remain what I am . . . I miss O.E.,† he understood these things all too well – he who was consumed in their flames."

The poetic counterpart to these intimate reflections is "Hamlet", the poem which was later to be read with such feeling over Pasternak's fresh grave. "Hamlet" was also dated 1946, like most of the other poems in the *Doctor Zhivago* cycle.

I repeat that in these and the following years, I met him far less frequently and there is much I can only piece together, with the aid of conjecture, from various things he told me during fleeting encounters over the whole period. Our meetings were always warm and cordial, and more than anything in my life I regret that they were so few and far between.

During these years a great new love entered his life.* He has spoken about it best of all in his own poetry – I learned infinitely more about it from this than from all the conflicting rumours then going round Moscow; I actually first saw the woman who inspired it only at his funeral. In the same letter of November 26, 1946, quoted above, he referred to it in the following way: "In contrast to all the changing tides of the last few years, my personal life has once more quite abruptly taken on a happy complexion."

Some time at the beginning of the winter of 1946 I was travelling in the Metro, gripping one of the metal handles overhead and reading in my newspaper a dispatch from Paris

† i.e. Osip Emilyevich Mandelstam.

about the results of the elections, in which the Communists had gained more votes than any other party, when suddenly I heard my name: "Alexander Konstantinovich!" I immediately recognized the voice of Pasternak. He was going only as far as the next station. I asked him how he was getting on, and he replied: "I am working, which is what matters." When someone answers the question in this vein, it generally means things are in pretty poor shape. He added that he was writing his novel and had finished "a good article" on his translations of Shakespeare* – this is exactly how he put it: a "good" article, but it was said quite unaffectedly, without a trace of self-satisfaction. He was also about to start a long article on Blok.* Taking off his glove, he shook hands with me and got out at Revolution Square. I watched as he walked away down the platform and saw that he was still wearing the same old *shuba* as in Chistopol, now very shabby, but that he had a new, tall hat made of seal-skin. As though sensing that I was looking at him, he turned round and smiled back at me, showing his white teeth. He was the youngest of all his contemporaries . . .

From the beginning of 1947, I frequently met the critic T.* We were both keen book collectors and carried on a lively barter in rare items. T. was a fervent admirer of Pasternak and kept thick files where he stored clippings of every article in which his name was so much as mentioned. This did not, however, prevent T. from joining in all the concerted campaigns of criticism against Pasternak, and he did so with superb shamelessness, never seeming to experience the slightest pangs of conscience. After publishing some reproving piece about Pasternak, he would ring him up a few days later and beg for copies of his latest poems. Strange to say, Pasternak took a lenient view of T., crediting him with some peculiar kind of unfathomable depth and subtlety which in actual fact he did not possess at all. It cannot be denied, however, that T. was very catholic in his tastes: this most fiercely strict upholder of "Socialist Realism" in poetry once sat with me for several hours delightedly reading out the verse of Sologub. If anyone had ever called T. a hypocrite to his face, he would have been genuinely shocked. For him the world was like a chess board divided into black and white squares and he knew the rules of the game to perfection: one piece could move only over white, and another only over black, and without harbouring the slightest doubt as to the validity of this scheme of things, he did his best to play both colours as skilfully as possible – something in which, for the most part, he succeeded very well, yet never losing his reputation as a splendid fellow. There is no doubt that he sincerely loved poetry of any kind. He was a born eclectic. Somewhere in his heart of hearts he was convinced that whatever he might *write* about its author, good verse would live on for ever, while the distress caused by his public attacks on it would soon pass away and be forgotten. This is indeed precisely what happened: T. is now dead and is remembered quite fondly by everyone. He was by no means unique as a psychological specimen. In those years I knew another man who took a deep and serious interest in religious philosophy. Since the rare works (Florenski, Fedorov, etc.) he needed for his studies were issued to readers in the Lenin Library only if they had a special permit certifying that they wanted them for "scientific purposes", he went and got a job with the atheist newspaper *Bezbozhnik** – this was before the war – in order to obtain the necessary piece of paper authorizing him to read these forbidden books, ostensibly because he required them for his work as an anti-religious propagandist.

It was from T. that I first got copies of new poems by Pasternak grouped together under the general title *Poems from a Novel in Prose*. Among them were "Hamlet", "In Holy Week", "Explanation", "Christmas Star" and one or two more. T. spoke of them with breathless admiration: he knew what was what in poetry. I could see at once that they marked the beginning of the new manner for which Pasternak had been searching in the previous years – simple, but not poverty-stricken, natural, but also containing imagery of a new kind. T. was not in the least put off by the use of Gospel themes, he accepted them in just the same way as he accepted classical mythology in Pushkin or Tiutchev – that is, as obvious conventions whose effect was to enhance and enrich the poetry without obliging the reader to believe in all those innumerable gods. "It's a myth, like any other", said T., as he recited Pasternak's new poems with the greatest relish. But already then I sensed that this was not a case of replacing one set of myths by another, but something far more significant.

I was very soon to see the reason why Pasternak had resorted to these Gospel motifs. Paradoxical though it may seem, it was his way of turning towards life, of protesting against the inhuman cult of Stalin, of renouncing his own disdainful aloofness of the poet in the ivory tower – in other words, of breaking out of the spiritual isolation to which his artistic independence condemned him. Old Bolsheviks in the forced labour camps found solace in their memories of Lenin and the early days of the Party. It gave them the strength to go on living – I saw this with my own eyes and am not speaking from hearsay. Others retreated into a shell of cynical fatalism, into extreme individualism, or into a neo-Darwinist philosophy of adaptation for the sake of survival. These were the ones who still had minds of their own. But all the others, the vast majority, simply lived from day to day, some of them – the most slow-witted – genuinely believing everything that had been dinned into their heads, and the rest just pretending to. It was important to have some kind of faith. People need faith at least as much as they need refrigerators or radio sets: life is bleak and bare without spiritual comfort.

It was Pasternak's great humanity, his instinctive, self-nurtured sense of democracy, his need for the warmth of human companionship and for simplicity in his mode of life, as well as the supreme lessons taught him by everything he loved and acknowledged in art that led him to the poetry of his later years, with its distinctive religiosity, and to the experience of writing his novel, *Doctor Zhivago*. It is tragic that this was not properly understood and that it was all interpreted quite differently. Even more tragic, perhaps, is the fact that his novel was not an unqualified success from the literary point of view and rendered his impeccable moral stance vulnerable in a way that made it possible for many people to speak condescendingly of him (quite apart from the abuse hurled at him by his out-and-out ill-wishers).

At the beginning of March 1947, people again started mentioning Pasternak's name at various meetings of the Union of Soviet Writers. At a conference of young authors Fadeyev made a sharp attack on him. Abusive references kept cropping up here and there – these were straws in the wind, and well before the article about him in *Culture and Life** it was clear enough that a new campaign against him was in the offing. The publication of this article was preceded by some direct interventions by Stalin himself in matters of art and history (his reply to Professor Razin in *Bolshevik** criticizing the Leninist view of the nature of war; the treatment of Eisenstein and Cherkasov, and the reaffirmation of the cult of Ivan the Terrible;* the denunciation of Leonov's play *The Golden Carriage*). As was always the case, these cues from on high were at once taken up and carried further at lower levels. A few days before the appearance of the *Culture and Life* article, I happened to run into Pasternak at the writers' savings bank in Lavrushinski Street. He looked gloomy and was in a visibly nervous state. Who could know where it might all end? We knew that after their expulsion from the Union of Writers, Akhmatova and Zoshchenko had even had their ration cards taken from them. Books by them which had already been set up in type were pulped down to the last copy. Later on Akhmatova, as a pensioner, was again issued with a ration card of sorts, but of Zoshchenko it was rumoured that he had gone back to one of the many professions he had practised during the years of the Civil War and was now making women's shoes.

At last the article attacking Pasternak appeared – on March 22, to be precise. I had also waited for it on tenterhooks, but when I read it, I could breathe easily again: with all its dishonesty and deliberate obtuseness, it did not amount to a definite "excommunication". It was clear that for the time being at least the question of throwing him out of the Union of Writers would not arise.

It was an early and very warm spring. On April 4 I ran into Pasternak on the Kamenny Bridge. He was in his *shuba* and had a strange yellow hat on his head. The ice was breaking up on the Moscow River. As always, he was friendly, but somehow ill-at-ease. I suspected he was tired of hearing expressions of sympathy, so I decided not to raise the subject, though later on I reproached myself for not having thought of something warm and heartening to say.

He did not get off scot-free: the edition of his selected verse which had already been set up in type was destroyed.* A few copies survived by some miracle. T., of course, was able to lay his hands on one and showed it to me triumphantly. This time he had so far refrained from writing an attack on Pasternak, but he was clearly in rather a panicky state over it – he said that the editor of the journal for which he worked was putting pressure on him to come out with something.

A. Vertinski, who shortly before all this had returned to Russia from emigration, met Pasternak somewhere and made some kind of plaintive comment which provoked a very sharp answer. On April 20, I again saw Pasternak in Lavrushinski Street, and asked him whether what people were saying about his clash with Vertinski was true. He said it was, and began to speak of Vertinski in an angry tone which I would never have expected from him – this was something quite new and unfamiliar in Pasternak as far as I was concerned. On this occasion too neither of us mentioned the *Culture and Life* attack on him, but he referred to it obliquely by saying: "At least they're not going to let me starve – I have been sent a contract for *Faust* . . ."*

One day at the end of June, I was sitting in the Alexandrovski Garden* reading a book when I saw someone approaching from the far end. He was dressed in a strange sand-coloured raincoat made from some kind of stiff, rough-looking material. Everybody was looking at him – it was a hot day for anyone to be wearing a coat. When this strange figure got closer I recognized Pasternak and called out to him. He smiled, came over and sat down close to me. It was on the tip of my tongue to suggest he might feel better without his coat on, but I refrained. Ten minutes later, in fact, he suddenly realized himself how hot he was and took it off. We sat for more than two hours, talking about various things, in that part of the garden which faces the embankment. There were very few people here – mothers and nannies with children, old men walking their dogs, and dreamy-looking girls sitting all by themselves with books. I remember the dappled patterns made by the sunlight coming through the thick leaves on the trees, the laughter and shouts of playing children and the thump of balls bouncing on the ground. I mentioned to Pasternak that I had seen the poems from his novel, and I tried to convey my feelings about them. I asked how the novel itself was going. That evening, as was my longstanding habit, I noted down some of what he said during this conversation:

"No – I am not by any means saying I am for giving up originality of expression, but I aim at a kind of originality which is unobtrusive, concealed in a simple and familiar form, restrained and unassuming – so that the subject matter is absorbed by the reader without his even noticing. I dream of a form by virtue of which the reader becomes, so to speak, one's co-author – an inconspicuous style in which nothing intervenes between the idea of a thing and its depiction . . ."

"Inspiration is something that comes when you are working at fever pitch and means the eclipse of the artist by his state of mind. It is a condition in which the mode of expression races ahead of the thought, in which the task is outpaced by the process of its accomplishment, and the answer springs to mind even before the question has been put. It is in the nature of language to create beauty of its own accord – a beauty which can neither be foreseen nor conceived beforehand. After writing in a burst of inspiration, you are later astonished – you at once recognize the result as your own work, but feel outdistanced by it."

"History is life's answer to the challenge of death – it is the conquest of death with the help of memory and time. History is naturally a product of the Christian era. Before it there were only myths, which are anti-historical by their very nature. The prime feature of the Christian era is that it fixed historical events in time. Myths are outside time . . ."

"History could also be described as a parallel universe created by mankind in response to an instinctive wish to hold death and non-being at bay. Time and memory – that is, history – are what constitute true immortality, for which the Christian idea of personal life everlasting is a poetic image . . ."

"I am not in the least worried by this talk of anti-Semitism which sometimes seems to start up quite suddenly – probably because I regard complete assimilation as the best possible thing for the Jews. The theory of race is quite specious and is needed only to justify odious practice. Try to explain the mulatto Pushkin* from a racist or extreme nationalist viewpoint!"

"When things are hard for me, I am saved by my ordinary daily round, by household chores, working in the garden out at Peredelkino . . ."

"For me the greatest boon is a life absorbed in the life of everybody else around me. I have never experienced happiness without feeling the urge to share it with somebody else – and the greater the happiness, the larger the number of people I wanted to share it with. It is from this – sometimes overpowering – urge that art is born . . ."

"In art it is just as important to unlearn as to learn. Otherwise it gradually becomes master over you. Perhaps what I call 'unlearning' is an even harder process than the acquisition of some aptitude or other. If I now write badly from my new point of view, I know this is because I have still not gone far enough in unlearning the kind of thing I was good at before . . ."

"When you are busy with a major piece of work and are totally wrapped up in it, it goes on taking shape even when you are at rest or asleep. You just have to know how to let yourself be carried along by the flow of it. This is not so simple. Sometimes, out of a rationalist mistrust of everything unconscious, instead of allowing yourself to drift along with a current more powerful than yourself, you begin to try and swim against it, wasting your strength on needless effort . . ."

"We do not know how to learn from the terrible experience contained in the biographies of our favourite poets and writers. Just fancy if Pushkin had persuaded Natalia Niko-layevna to retire to Mikhailovskoye with him* and he had lived on there for many years, scratching away with his quill pen and throwing logs into the crackling stoves – what a marvellous thing that would have been for Russia, and for us all! We never learn the lessons of others and we are all prone to plunge into giddy excitements that can only bring us to grief. But it is only in an ordinary kind of life that one can find happiness and the right conditions for work. Do you remember Chistopol? I always look back on it with pleasure . . ."

I said I thought it was probably the hardest thing in the

world to learn from other people's experience, and he readily agreed:

"Yes . . . Each man is a Faust in his own way – he has to go through and experience everything himself . . ."

"Any advance in human knowledge can only arise through a spirit of contradiction, by virtue of what I call the law of repulsion, or the need to disprove fallacies and correct long-established errors. The same kind of advance in art generally starts from an attempt to follow in someone's footsteps, from a need to pay homage to an object of intense admiration . . ."

"There is something false and spurious about a writer setting himself up as a teacher of life. Compare the unassuming straightforwardness of Pushkin and Chekhov, their simplicity, their innocence and modest devotion to work, with the frantic concern of Gogol, Dostoyevski and Tolstoi about the tasks facing the world and their own mission in it. For me this is pretentiousness – I find it offensive and it prevents me from enjoying them as writers. The highest a writer can achieve is that his personal life – the life he leads for himself and not for show or for others – should serve as a worthy model without any deliberate effort or grand flourishes on his part. I have always been put off by the element of sheer ostentation in Tolstoyanism . . ."

"The second-hand nature of copybook sentiments is no guarantee of their being common to all mankind."

"We are made to rejoice at what brings us unhappiness, to declare our love for things we do not love, to behave in direct contradiction to our own instinct for the truth. And we stifle this instinct. We lie to ourselves and, like slaves, idealize our lack of freedom . . ."

"I started to work on my novel again when I saw that all

our rosy expectations of the changes the end of the war was supposed to bring to Russia were not being fulfilled. The war itself was like a cleansing storm, like a breeze blowing through an unventilated room. Its sorrows and hardships were not as bad as the inhuman lie – they shook to its core the power of everything specious and unorganic to the nature of man and society which has gained such a hold over us. But the dead weight of the past was too strong. The novel is absolutely essential for me as a way of expressing my feelings. One cannot sit with folded arms. A man is responsible for his life and everything that has been given him. I remember what an unshakeable optimist you were too during the war, and I even argued with you – though sometimes I wanted to believe you were right . . ."

I said nothing, and he went on. I could see he was talking about things he had brooded on for a long time and felt very strongly about. Next he spoke of the role of tradition in art, the tradition without which there can be no culture:

"The grand traditions of the great Russian novel, of Russian poetry and drama, express the living features of the Russian spirit as it took shape historically in the course of the last century. To rebel against them is to condemn yourself to something forced, artificial and unorganic. *War and Peace*, *A Dreary Story** and *The Idiot* are just as much features of Russia as the birch-trees and the quietly-flowing rivers. There is no point in trying to cultivate palm trees in Peredelkino – even Michurin wouldn't have gone in for that. Our literature is the concentrated spiritual experience of the nation, and to ignore it means to start all over again from nothing . . ."

"I have been re-reading Pushkin a great deal. His letters are marvellous – what a complete lack of affectation and what an ability to be himself! It is quite astonishing when you think how clearly he understood his own importance, and the value he himself put on his work in 'Monument'* . . ."

"I like the Russian literature of the first half of the nineteenth century, and that of the second half of the twentieth . . ."

"Tragedy is founded on the idea of free will. If a man is able to choose a particular solution or course of action among several different ones offered by life, he then has a sense of moral or some other kind of responsibility towards history or the truth. When one is not enabled to weigh possible alternatives, there can be no tragedy. The right to choose one's path is the modern lot – to use the word without any suggestion of fatalism . . ."

"It may seem odd, but fatalism or political mysticism became the characteristic feature of those who called themselves 'materialists' . . ."

A little girl nearby hit Pasternak with her ball just at a moment when he was particularly carried away by what he was saying. He stopped in confusion. I picked up the ball and threw it after the little girl, who ran away laughing. After this the conversation veered off into matters of no importance. I glanced unthinkingly at my watch. Pasternak saw me do so and began to apologize for "keeping" me. We both got up and started walking towards the way out. He carried his outlandish raincoat on his arm. We said goodbye at the foot of the steps up to the bridge. Before walking off he said to me:

"We do not meet very often nowadays, but we always talk as though we had seen each other only the day before . . ."

For the rest of the day I kept thinking about his novel, the concept of which had grown extraordinarily in my eyes as a result of our conversation. I had wanted to ask him about many other things – the place of the poems in the novel, the structure of the whole work, and whether there would be an autobiographical element in the plot, but a conversation with Pasternak was rarely a dialogue, and I had not been able to bring myself to interrupt him.

During the whole second half of that year I worked very hard and at the beginning of the winter two Moscow theatres started rehearsals of my new play. It somehow happened that as I was talking with the director of one of these theatres, we got on to the subject of Pasternak's Shakespeare translations. I spoke of *Antony and Cleopatra* in such glowing terms that the director expressed great eagerness to read it. I offered to get a copy – which I did by phoning Pasternak and asking him to send me a typescript. After this it was suggested that Pasternak himself should be invited to read his translation to the company of the theatre in question. At first I was the only go-between, but later, in order to make the whole thing sound a little more convincing in practical terms I managed to involve the theatre's literary adviser in the business and Pasternak eagerly fell in with the idea – only he was very insistent that I should attend, so there would be "someone close to me", as he put it, at the reading. Needless to say, I had fully intended to be there in any case.

The reading was fixed for January 30, 1948. A blizzard was blowing that evening – the janitors were having a hard time trying to clear away the snow in front of the buildings, and the city's transport was not working too well. Even the theatre performances were starting late.

All the members of the company who were not appearing on stage that night gathered in the spacious office of the theatre's chief producer. I waited for Pasternak in the foyer, near the entrance. He came in holding his hat in his hands and using it to brush the snow off his collar and sleeves. After greeting me he asked anxiously whether I thought it was all right that he had asked three of his friends to come along to the reading as well. I set his mind at rest, and asking the doorman to direct his friends backstage when they arrived, I took Pasternak to the office and introduced him to those already waiting there. On the way he said to me: "Well, you are doing very well again – I read what *Evening Moscow* had to say about your play . . . but it really is completely deserved" – he added innocently, in case I might be offended. In those years to be "doing well" was not always a good criterion of a person's worth. I smiled to myself at his reassuring afterthought. Soon his friends duly turned up: there were two women I did not know (one of whom, as I now think, was Ivinskaya, but I am not sure), and the inevitable A. E. Kruchenykh, whom I had known for ages.

Pasternak was in excellent spirits, very friendly and courteously attentive to everybody. An usherette brought in a tray for the water carafe but dropped it. Pasternak, who was at the other end of the room, rushed to pick it up. Others followed his example and for a moment there was bedlam round the tray lying on the floor. By now everybody had come who was expected, and we all started sitting down. Pasternak called me over and said in a low voice: "Please sit a little closer to me!" – this meant that he was after all rather on edge. I took a place almost next to him at the desk where he sat.

He read only extracts, giving detailed summaries with comments of everything he missed out, and, as usual, wandering away from the point and even speculating on certain things – not that all this was any less interesting in itself. He also made his customary attempt to ham it up a little in the comic bits and became touchingly emotional in the tragic scenes. The actors looked on as though in the presence of some kind of prodigy and were more interested in him than in Shakespeare's play, but he did not notice this. His hair was already noticeably grey, but still silvery rather than white and he looked just as young as ever for his fifty-seven years – a vigorous, agile man. During his commentaries he twice turned to me, as though for confirmation of what he was saying.

After the reading was over, somebody in the back row asked him to recite some of his own verse. He was clearly pleased by the request, but at first he pretended to be reluctant – even his false modesty, however, was utterly charming, quite unlike anyone else's. It turned out that he had brought with him a folder containing his new poems, and at last he agreed to read them, but only after a five-minute break.

During the break he went over to talk with his friends, while I mingled with the actors. They were all full of "ohs" and "ahs" – and quite captivated by him. The usual thing during the interval at the reading of a play was for the actors to start discussing who would take which role, but on this occasion the only talk was about Pasternak. Neither Antony and Cleopatra, nor Shakespeare could compete with him that evening!

After the interval, when everybody had returned to their places in the producer's office, Pasternak again put up a show of resistance and tried to cry off. But everybody understood perfectly well that the main proceedings were just about to begin and loudly egged him on. During all this friendly wrangling, he suddenly turned to me at one moment and asked whether I had got my telephone back again (it had taken a long time to have it re-installed after its removal during the war). I still cannot imagine what he meant by asking me this – perhaps it was his oblique way of expressing his gratitude to me for having been so faithful to him – even if only at a distance for the most part.

Before beginning to read, he spoke about his novel and its hero – a doctor who after his death leaves behind a manuscript with his poems. Then he read "Winter Night" ("The Candle Burned"). He was visibly rather worked-up. Next he read "March", "In Holy Week", "Christmas Star", "The Miracle", and some others.* The actors applauded wildly. Pasternak no longer bothered to look at his manuscript and recited "Hamlet" from memory ("The Miracle", too, he had recited without his manuscript). The way he spoke "Hamlet" is quite unforgettable. It was a confession, a self-revelation . . . After reading "Christmas Star" he talked about the genesis of the poem, somehow connecting it with the influence of Blok.

His warm reception by the theatre company touched him in a way that was affecting and yet a little pathetic. As I sat there I couldn't help thinking how very lonely he must be if he needed such simple triumphs as this . . .

He was asked to read one of the poems again, and he said he was willing to repeat any of them. There were shouts of "The Candle Burned", "Hamlet"! I would have liked him to read "Hamlet" again, but he chose "The Candle Burned" and I immediately understood that there would never be any encore for this self-revelation.

As he read again, his voice was somehow especially gentle:

> Snow swept over the earth,
> Swept it from end to end.
> The candle on the table burned,
> The candle burned . . .

How could one explain the strength of these utterly un-pretentious words? Was it a case of Lermontov's "There are words whose meaning . . ."* or of what Pasternak him-self once defined as "unheard-of simplicity"* – the heresy which would bring down merciless retribution on his head? But it makes no sense to cudgel one's brains over a miracle instead of just listening in grateful admiration:

> . . . On the bright ceiling
> Fell the shadows
> Of crossed hands, crossed feet,
> Crossed fate.
> Two shoes fell to the floor
> With a thud.
> From the night-light
> Wax tears dropped on a frock . . .

In front of him he held a sheet of paper with the poem typed on it, but he did not look at it:

> . . . And everything was lost
> In the white-haired, snowy darkness.
> The candle burned . . .

I listened to Pasternak's familiar voice with its deep, nasal timbre and long-drawn-out vowels, and it seemed to me that the poem could only be recited thus, only by this voice, and only on a snowy winter night, with a blizzard blowing, as now . . .

All the actors crowded round him. I went and stood some way off, but I could hear the fulsome and banal compliments pronounced in well-practised voices – though I had no doubt that they were sincerely meant: actors are quite capable of giving way to their feelings.

After shaking a dozen hands or so, Pasternak broke away from the circle round him and, seeing me, came over again and asked – I no longer remember his exact words – what I had thought of it all. What could I say? I mumbled something about how I had recently read, for the first time in my life, the prose of Marina Tsvetayeva, compared the evening's experience with this, and said something vaguely to the effect that it had been "a red letter day". Suddenly he embraced me, kissed me awkwardly on the cheek near the ear and repeated several times over: "Thank you, thank you!" The actors looked at us with respectful incomprehension.

Pasternak's friends appeared in the passageway and I hastily said goodbye and hurried out, as though afraid of losing a single drop of everything that was brimming over inside me . . .

At the end of May I again met Pasternak in our writers' savings bank. He was in a white panama hat and light-coloured suit, looking young and handsome. For some time now there had been rumours about his new and serious love affair. We went out together and stood for a while in the entrance of the building on Lavrushinski Street.

He said he had recently read the completed first part of his novel for four solid hours to Anna Akhmatova while she was on a visit from Leningrad. "I wore her out so much that she almost had an attack of angina . . ." He was in a jaunty mood and the conversation did not move beyond a few light-hearted pleasantries. He asked me when the première of my new play would be. I told him the rehearsals had dragged on interminably and it would probably be put on only at the beginning of the next season. "Invite me without fail!" he said. "Of course, Boris Leonidovich!" He went inside.

In my diary I have the following entry under September 19: "The golden autumn has given way to cold and rain. The manuscript of the first half of Pasternak's novel is going round the city. I shall have it in a few days' time: T. has promised to get it for me."

But on October 1, 1948 – the day of the dress rehearsal of my play – I was arrested. The première did not take place.

4

At the end of the summer of 1954, among the first of the great wave of "rehabilitated" prisoners let out of the camps, I returned to Moscow after an absence of almost six years. And before long in the same writers' savings bank in Lavrushinski Street where we had last met, I saw Pasternak again. As I went in he was filling out a cheque at the counter. When I spoke to him, he turned round, looked closely at me, recognized me and embraced me warmly. "I had heard, I had heard you were back," he said, without lowering his voice and paying not the slightest attention to all the other people round about. "And here am I – still 'uncorrected'* ..."

We went out together. I told him how that spring I had read his poems in *Znamia*.* This was the cycle entitled *Poems from the novel Doctor Zhivago* – the first verse of his, I believe, to be published in all these years.* The one-volume edition of his poems, which he had given me during the war with such a kind dedication, had been sent out to me in the camp from home, and I had kept it by me throughout my years of imprisonment. I had usually got up earlier than everybody else in the barracks in order to read it in the mornings, and if ever something prevented me from doing so, I always felt as though I had not washed. "Oh, if only I had known this then, in those black years!" he said, "life would have been so much more bearable just to think that I was *out there* too ..."

Looking at him now I had the impression that he had

hardly aged at all.

*

In the years after this, we met briefly several times, often just long enough to say hello or exchange a few words on matters of no particular importance. On one such occasion, he said he had seen a poster advertising resumed performances of *Long, Long Ago* at the Central Soviet Army Theatre . . . "You see what a good prophet I am: so many changes everywhere – and in our lives as well – but your girl-hussar is careering around the stage again just as before . . . but," he added wistfully, "I still have no luck with the theatre." "How lucky *we* have been on the other hand!" I replied, "after the Arts Theatre production of your translation of *Maria Stuart*, you wrote 'Bacchanalia', didn't you?" "So you already know it?" he said with a smile, "and you must have noticed, of course, that it is contrary to everything I have written either before or since." He seemed quite astonished by my enthusiasm for "Bacchanalia".* I said that the poem, long and complex though it was, seemed to have been written at one go, at a single sitting, without pausing for breath. "It is good if it creates such an impression," he replied, "though it was not quite like that. I actually wrote it at more than one sitting, as I do most of my poems. But you are right: it took me by surprise, it came in a rush of what is generally called inspiration. You know how one sometimes keeps a bottle of home-made wine over winter in the attic – it could easily stay there for ages, but you happen to touch it accidentally and the cork suddenly flies out – well, for me this poem was like a cork flying out. I was astonished by it myself – but an even greater surprise has been that so many people like it so much . . ."

*

Among the manuscripts left after Pasternak's death was the

first part of a long play about a serf actress* which he wrote
in the very last years of his life, still cherishing the dream of
making his mark in the theatre. During this same meeting
(it was in Peredelkino), when I asked him what he was writing
now, he replied:

"For heaven's sake, don't think I am trying to be evasive,
but at the moment I am in one of those indeterminate phases
which is probably in fact the incubation period of something
new. All I can say is that I am thinking of a play again."

In a letter he wrote to me two years after this conversation
and less than a year before his death, Pasternak spoke as
follows about this major piece of work, which was in effect
the last he was to start on:

"The best you can wish me is that nothing unforeseen
should interfere with the progress, or prevent the completion
– still far away in the future – of the work which has now
seized hold of me. From the stage of inertia, in which the
idea of the play first came to me, it has entered the phase
in which an idle experiment has become an innermost
desire, turned into a passion . . ."

During several of our chance encounters, Pasternak urged
me to go out and visit him in Peredelkino, but I never once
took up his invitation. Apart from my natural diffidence,
there was also the constraint felt by most people who had
returned "from there". My formal "rehabilitation" had not
gone through straightaway. My plays were again being put
on in Moscow and Leningrad theatres, but my papers had
still not been regularized. There was some delay before I
was re-elected to membership of the Union of Soviet Writers
(though this had its advantages: it later saved me from
attending – or finding an excuse not to attend – the meeting
of Moscow writers at which the decision to expel Pasternak
was adopted*). All this inhibited me, and I just never brought
myself to go and see him. Furthermore, I was too fond of
Pasternak and valued his feelings for me too highly to risk
turning up there at an inopportune moment. Or perhaps the

truth of the matter is that I was not so much shying away from a visit as putting it off to a more settled time – which in fact never came.

On August 18, 1957 I went out to Peredelkino to see some friends and ran into Pasternak as I was crossing the bridge over the river. He was dressed in something that looked like pyjamas, or a light summer suit – white with dark blue stripes. His hair was now quite grey, but his face was as young as ever. He greeted me in very friendly fashion. At first we talked standing at the side of the main road by the bridge. He was a familiar figure in Peredelkino and everybody looked at us as they passed – though few, as a matter of interest, gave any sign of recognition. He suggested we go for a little walk. I forgot I was expected for lunch, and went off with him.

I remember everything just as if it were yesterday – the light-grey waters of the lake with the purplish-pink glint on them, the embankment with its branchy willows and the black-edged white posts going all the way round, the beautiful old lime trees, cedars and larches in the surviving part of the former estate to which Pasternak took me, and his beloved voice, with the intonation I knew so well. He showed me the old house, with the colonnade – once the estate of the Samarins, as described in his poem "The Old Park". In his student days Pasternak was friendly with one of the young Samarins – in his *An Essay in Autobiography* he gives a brief account of the strange and sad fate of Dmitri Samarin. Dmitri Samarin was evidently also the real-life original of Yuri Zhivago, at least as far as the biographical externals go.

We strolled around for about two hours and talked of many different things – or rather, as in former days, Pasternak talked while I listened.

His manner of talking too had not changed – that is, his sentences piled up rapidly in dense, urgent clusters, he interrupted himself, wandered off into digressions before getting back to the subject – always seeming to lose the thread of what he was saying until you got used to it and understood the relentless logic behind it. He seemed rather agitated and in need of relieving his feelings.

I have to admit that at first I thought he must be exaggerating in many respects. On that beautiful summer morning in the peaceful, familiar countryside near Moscow his forebodings of troubles and persecutions to come seemed to me the product of excessive imagination. A year and two months later I understood that it was not he who had been over-apprehensive but I who had been too complacent. Actually, I first learned of many of the things that were going on only during this conversation.

He told me that the storm clouds were gathering over him. His novel was shortly going to appear in Italy. He had meant to stop publication there, but for some reason had not done so, or no longer could: "I do not now have the right to," as he put it. The previous year it had been turned down by *Novy Mir*. Kotov had been going to publish it in the State Publishing House for Literature, *Goslitizdat*, but had died, and the rest of the people there had no time at all for it – they were too busy with their petty careerist scheming. In the Union of Writers the novel had been labelled "counter-revolutionary". "If it were so," he said, "I would not be afraid to admit it, but it isn't true." He backed up his point with a simile:

"It is just as though you were to define this cedar here only by reference to the fact that it is blocking out the sun with the shadow in which we are standing . . ."

"They want to make a new Zoshchenko of me . . . Yes they do, I assure you. No, there's nothing to be done about it now; the order from above has already been given. On Friday I was summoned to a meeting of the Secretariat [of the Union of Writers]. It was supposed to be a meeting behind closed doors, but I didn't go and they took great offence and passed a fearful resolution denouncing me. Some of them are going out of their way to inflate the whole thing and heighten the tension – K., for instance. Even Panferov is taking it more calmly than K. and his like. I suddenly find I have a lot of enemies. At this meeting of the Secretariat, by the way, they appointed a committee to have things out with me . . . No, no – don't you believe it, I'm in for trouble this time: my turn has come. You really have no idea – it's a very complicated business, involving the pride and prestige of all kinds of people. It's a clash of rival authorities. The novel itself is hardly at issue – most of the people concerned with the matter haven't even read it. A few of them would gladly just drop the whole affair – not out of sympathy for me, mind you, only because they want to avoid a public scandal. But this is no longer possible. I'm told that some-body at the meeting accused me of being hungry for pub-licity, of wanting to create a great hullabaloo and scandal. If only they knew how foreign and hateful I find such things! I sometimes wake up feeling horror and misery at myself, at this unfortunate character of mine that demands total freedom of the spirit, and at this sudden turn of events in my life which is so distressing for those close to me."

I tried to change the subject, and we got on to Tvardovski's recent conversation with Khrushchev – about the writers, whom they divided like birds, into those used for hunting, and those valued for their song, and many other things.

I remembered that in my notebook I had a copy of the photograph taken in 1936 of him, Meyerhold and myself. I gave it to him. He thanked me, but wanted to know whether I had another copy:

"I can never keep anything – I shall lose this as well. How well Meyerhold comes out! And how much you have changed – though I remember you still like this in Chistopol . . ."

(He was right about not being able to keep things. A little while later I happened to meet Kruchenykh who offered to let me have this very same photograph. On going into the matter, I found he had got it from a woman friend of Pasternak's who had begged him to give it to her.)

I had the impression that after our two hours' walk and conversation he was very much calmer – perhaps because of being able to get out everything that was on his mind to someone he was used to confiding in.

As we said goodbye he again urged me to come and visit him: "Just drop in any Sunday after 1 o'clock . . ." Thinking that the invitation was made out of his usual graciousness, I did not avail myself of it, even though there were many things I wanted to ask him about.

A few months before this, I had read his *An Essay in Autobiography*. Kazakievich had been going to publish it in the third volume of *Literary Moscow* and the manuscript was lent to me for a short time by one of the editors – perhaps by Kazakievich himself, I no longer remember.*

Brilliantly written, with the tautly compressed intellectual energy typical of the best of Pasternak's later prose-writing (not all of *Doctor Zhivago*, unfortunately, is written like this), it struck me by its narrow focus, by the way in which the author's vast and varied literary experience is somehow deliberately whittled down.

An Essay in Autobiography is not a rehash of *Safe Conduct*, or a sequel to it, but rather runs parallel to it, as a kind of musical variation. There is a studied dryness, a marked severity about those judgements that contradict his previous views (particularly in what he says about Mayakovski, for instance). He leaves out many things which certainly affected his development – some of them even I was a witness to (the war, Shakespeare, Chistopol and others) – as though selecting out of his life only those parts which led up to the writing of *Doctor Zhivago*, omitting or passing over in silence everything else, harshly and unjustly condemning in their entirety important and fruitful periods in his earlier work. There is, however, nothing new about this in Russian literature – one only has to think of Gogol, or Tolstoi's ambiguous feelings about the great novels which made his name (indeed *War and Peace* was even explicitly disowned by him). In this sense Pasternak was only following tradition by donning a hairshirt and renouncing his early poems.

On the whole *An Essay in Autobiography*, with its highly subjective, undoubtedly sincere and agonized re-appraisal of himself – which naturally entailed, by the law of resonance, re-appraisal of all earlier influences, predilections and affinities – seemed to me to impoverish in some way, and even to distort the image of the Pasternak whom I had known and loved for so many years. I sensed behind all this a kind of defiance, the defiance of a very lonely, desperate writer who had grown tired of his own loneliness and despair. Furthermore, there was here, I felt, the longing of the man of letters for action – something else familiar to us from the case of Tolstoi.

I am not sure I would have dared speak my mind about this to Pasternak himself, even though he had earlier always reacted very simply whenever I argued with him. From various indications I had reason to think that in recent years he had become less indulgent and forbearing than earlier, perhaps out of sheer tiredness. There were now stories in literary circles about brusque behaviour that would have been unthinkable previously. This was a different Pasternak from the one I had known. The earlier one would scarcely have reacted so crossly to V. Vishnevski's vulgar and offensive toast.*

At the end of the year I saw Pasternak again at a performance of *Faust* by the visiting Hamburg Theatre. His novel had already come out in Italian and during the interval he was mobbed by a crowd of foreign newspapermen. One of them thrust a copy of his own translation of *Faust* into his hand and they all started taking photographs. The earlier Pasternak would have thought it an unseemly comedy, but this new Pasternak stood there obediently in the foyer of the theatre, posing book in hand before the journalists while the flash-bulbs popped away. He evidently thought he *had* to do this for some reason or other, since I cannot imagine it gave him any pleasure. He had been overtaken by world fame, but seemed none the happier for it – one could see the strain in the awkward way he stood there, and in the expression on his face. He looked more of a martyr than a conquering hero. There was something demeaning about it all. I wanted to go up to him, but changed my mind and left the theatre with a strange and disagreeable feeling of unease.

As everybody knows, the manuscript of the novel was given by Pasternak to the Milan publisher and Communist Feltrinelli with the knowledge of *Novy Mir* and *Goslitizdat*,* but on condition that it came out in Italy only after publication in the Soviet Union – which was actually being prepared; it had been announced as forthcoming in a journal, and Pasternak was already working on it with an editor from *Goslitizdat*. There was, therefore, nothing "disloyal" about the arrangement with Feltrinelli. The situation only took on an awkward turn when it became clear that there was no question of the novel being published in the Soviet Union in the near future. In the meantime the Italian translation had been completed. To Feltrinelli's anxious enquiries Pasternak first replied with a telegram telling him to proceed as he thought fit, but later, after pressure had been put on him, he cabled again asking Feltrinelli to wait. But since there was no mention of how long he was supposed to wait, or any other kind of stipulation, Feltrinelli decided to take his cue from the first telegram and go ahead. In October 1957, a group of Soviet poets went to Italy. Pasternak had been among those invited, but his place was taken by Surkov who evidently made an attempt to recover the manuscript from Feltrinelli. It is said that Togliatti was the intermediary between them. But Feltrinelli was not to be swayed and the novel came out in Milan shortly afterwards.

The first edition sold out in a matter of hours. During the winter, spring and summer of 1958, the novel appeared in other languages. The Soviet press kept silence until the late autumn of that year, when the storm at last broke.

It was thus not foreign publication of the novel that precipitated the campaign against Pasternak, but the award of the Nobel Prize – by which time a whole year had gone by since it had come out. This prolonged silence about the novel's appearance abroad was the first in a long series of blunders in the handling of the affair. The author could to some extent be held responsible for the novel itself, but scarcely for all the many foreign editions, commentaries and articles, and the award of the Nobel Prize. Not long before we had seen how Sartre had been awarded the prize over his own objections, so to blame Pasternak for getting the prize was just as unreasonable as it would have been to hold it against Sartre. Acceptance of the prize, moreover, had never been condemned by the Soviet Union in cases where it had been awarded to our scientists. It was clearly, then, not a question of disapproval of the prize as such, but only of its award in this particular instance. But why should Pasternak have been expected to renounce the prize when none of our physicists, medical researchers and biologists had ever done so?

The novel had been circulating in Moscow in manuscript copies for several years; it had been officially under consideration by Soviet publishers and there had been no announcement of its rejection by one of the journals – and it can happen, after all, that a work may be rejected by one publisher and accepted by another (as, for example, Kazakievich's *Blue Notebook*, not to mention many other works in recent years). What, then, was so criminal in Pasternak's case? There was nothing secretive or underhand here; it was all done quite openly, for everyone to see. The idea that Pasternak might be a candidate for the Nobel Prize had been mooted in literary circles abroad very much earlier, well before anything had been heard of *Doctor Zhivago*: there was serious talk of it already in 1947, when a group of English writers put up Pasternak's name for the prize.

News of this even reached Moscow. I remember an occasion in the autumn of 1947, at the house of a certain writer, when there was talk about it in the presence of Pasternak's first wife. Times were then very much harder and everybody there expressed concern at the effect such a move might have on Pasternak's position – almost in the same words he was to use himself in conversation with me ten years later: that he would be made into a "second Zoshchenko". It may well be that these rumours at that time played a part in the decision to pulp the volume of his poetry which had been due to appear in the series "Selected Works of Soviet Writers",* in just the same way as books by Akhmatova and Zoshchenko had been destroyed the year before.

In his conversation with me in August 1957, Pasternak had clearly foreseen what was in store for him and had not exaggerated in the slightest. Real poets often predict their own future in verse, and long before the grim autumn of 1958 he had written: "The darkness of the night is aimed at me / along the sights of a thousand opera glasses." The whole of this poem, "Hamlet", written twelve years before Pasternak's exclusion from the Union of Writers, is remarkable for its foreboding of his own fate – a foreboding which was to come true with a vengeance.

There are no grounds for thinking that Pasternak "wanted to suffer". There is all the difference in the world between knowing that something is inevitable and actually *wanting* it to come about. It is quite possible for someone to see, as a matter of cold fact, that a certain thing is inevitable and yet to do nothing to try and ward it off. This theme crops up twice in poems written by Pasternak after the war and later included in the novel. After the lines from "Hamlet" quoted above, he goes on: "Abba, Father, if it be possible, / let this cup pass from me" . . . This is the moral dilemma posed in one of the most beautiful of all traditions – the story of Christ praying in the garden of Gethsemane – and not for nothing is it the subject of a major poem by Pasternak:*

The night was a kingdom of annihilation,
Of non-being,
The whole world seemed uninhabited,
And only this garden was a place for the living.
He gazed into the black abyss,
Empty, without beginning or end.
Sweating blood, he prayed to his Father
That this cup should pass him by.

The verse is attributed by the author to the hero of his novel, Yuri Zhivago, but this is a little far-fetched since there is nothing in Zhivago's life to which it might be relevant. Here, in the voice of the novel's hero, it is in fact his living creator (but by no means his double) who is speaking: the author himself.

Yet didn't Pasternak want to have his novel published by *Novy Mir* and *Goslitizdat*? It might seem strange that he had any such hope. But this was in 1956, the year of the Twentieth Congress. Much was changing and new vistas were opening up. At such radical turning points, things that until a little while before would have been thought impossible could suddenly come to pass. When I first read *One Day in the Life of Ivan Denisovich* and *Matryona's Home** in manuscript I believed the odds were absolutely against their ever being published. Fortunately, I was wrong. *Doctor Zhivago* was "unprintable" only in a very relative sense – many of the ideas in it are expressed even more unequivocally in the long poem "A High Illness", which was actually republished several times during the Stalin years.

The whole meaning and substance of Pasternak's later years lay in the fact that, knowing his fate beforehand, he went towards it with open eyes and without illusions, doing what he rightly or wrongly considered to be his duty:

But the book of life has reached the page
Which is the most precious of all holy things.
What has been written must be fulfilled,
Let it be so. Amen.*

This "choice" or decision was not a simple one: to begin with, it conflicted with Pasternak's whole character – which was that of a gentle poet, trusting and open-hearted, completely unfanatical. Victor Shklovski wrote of him in his book *Zoo*: "He will live his whole life happily and loved by all." (In the edition of 1964 this phrase is omitted.) But the rough edges apparent in *An Essay in Autobiography* were a clear indication for me of the injuries and scars sustained by the poet in his struggle with himself. In 1936, in his poem "The Artist", he has the following lines:

> . . . But what is he then? In which arena
> Was his later wisdom won,
> With whom were his battles fought?
> Only with himself, only with himself . . .

One would like to quote the whole poem. The accuracy with which it foreshadows the future destiny of the poet himself now seems nothing short of miraculous. But true poetry is always miraculous – what would be its point otherwise?

> Exact to the hundredth
> Of every inch, I see
> Down forest cuttings my future
> Fulfilled for me.*

This he said with reference to his own life in one of his beautiful late poems about the Russian countryside, where he achieves a supreme poetic quality not merely by heightening the significance of the humble and simple natural scene through metaphors and similes, but by allowing nature itself to serve as an all-encompassing image – which it does without ever ceasing to be itself, a faithfully-drawn landscape.

His choice was not a simple one for the further reason that he could have no possible illusions: he had lost too many close friends and in the Stalin years had too often waited on some desolate night for the agents of Yezhov or Beria to knock on the gate of his house in Peredelkino. What saved Pasternak in those days? It is hard to say. All we know for certain is that in 1955 the young procurator R.*, who was going into the case of Meyerhold, was astonished to discover that Pasternak was still at liberty and had never been arrested: according to the papers in his hands Pasternak was marked down to figure as an "accomplice" in an imaginary conspiracy supposedly hatched by people connected with the arts, and for which both Meyerhold and Babel paid with their lives. Another name which cropped up fleetingly in this "case" was that of Yuri Olesha, who also in the upshot escaped arrest. The honest and conscientious young procurator was quite unversed in literary matters, and Pasternak's name only became widely known after the business of the Nobel Prize.

At some stage during the preparation of this infamous frame-up it was evidently decided to make do with Meyerhold and Babel, who had already been arrested, but even so, it is quite clear, judging by the materials in the "case", that Pasternak was in serious danger of arrest in the second half of 1939, and no doubt at other times too. When he was asked, much later on, in connection with Meyerhold's "rehabilitation", to state his view of Meyerhold's political outlook, he wrote briefly that Meyerhold had been far more Soviet than himself. This strikes a note both of bitter humour and of curious bravado, but fortunately he said it at a time when you could get away with such things.

All this does not mean that I completely accept the ideas and images in *Doctor Zhivago* or that I in any way share Pasternak's view of it as the major achievement of his life.

In the days when the novel was circulating round Moscow in manuscript I did not read it. For some reason I believed it would soon appear in print and made no effort to get hold of it, though this would not have been difficult – and Pasternak himself would have given it to me if I had asked. But I read it very much later, when all the stormy controversy

158

about it had died down and Pasternak himself was no longer alive.

Is it necessary for me to write about this? Yes, I think it is. I am writing about my encounters with Pasternak, and this too, in its way, was an encounter . . .

To put it briefly: the novel disappointed me. Not trusting my own judgement, as soon as I came to the end of it I at once started to read it all over again. Making up my mind about this book, by now famous, seemed to me to be a matter in which I owed myself a very serious responsibility. Apart from reading it twice, I came back to it many times, leafing through, looking again at certain chapters or pages, and carrying on a constant debate in my own mind both with Pasternak and myself.

I would even go so far as to say that this first encounter with the novel was dramatic for me: not only because of my great affection for Pasternak as a man and a poet, but also because the last thing I wanted was to join the ranks of those who attacked the novel without giving it proper thought (or even, in many cases, without bothering to read it at all). I shall always be infinitely grateful to Pasternak for everything I have received, and continue to receive from his poetry, but as he himself says somewhere in the novel, the greatest misfortune of our times is the inability of people to form their own opinions, and it is out of deference to him, therefore, that I have decided to set down my own thoughts about the novel, wherever they may lead me.

There are extraordinary pages in *Doctor Zhivago*, but how many more there would have been if Pasternak, instead of forcing himself to compose a *novel*, had simply written unconstrainedly, in wide-ranging fashion, about himself, his times and his life. Everything in the book that smacks of a novel is weak: people speak and act only as mouthpieces of the author; conversations between the main characters – all members of the intelligentsia – are either naive embodiments of the author's own thoughts clumsily dressed up as dialogue, or heavy-handed impersonations. All the scenes involving ordinary people (the train journey, the partisan camp, etc.) strike a false note – Pasternak simply had no ear for this kind of thing. The narrative devices are also naive, conventional, and forced, or have an artificial, derivative air about them. There is a noticeable influence of Dostoyevski – but the conversational duels in a Dostoyevski novel are real debates between adversaries placed on a footing of dialectical equality (as Bakhtin has brilliantly shown in his book), whereas all the main characters in *Doctor Zhivago* are simply distillations of Pasternak himself, differing only in the strength of the brew.

There is no broad picture of the era, in its many aspects, of the kind that might be expected in a work of epic scope. What we have is a moralistic (not even philosophical) discourse illustrated by material in narrative and descriptive form. He writes magnificently about nature, art and the process of composing verse: future students of Pasternak's poetry will find what he says on this subject indispensable. Also magnificent are many of the incidental thoughts and reflections (some of which I had already heard from him in conversation, though admittedly in a different form for the most part) and certain psychological portraits interspersed here and there. Then of course there are the poems, and one or two other things. But it doesn't add up to a great novel.

Even on a cursory reading one is struck by the number of times he repeats things he has said somewhere else before – not just ideas, but images. In *Safe Conduct*, for instance, he writes (on page 97) of Mayakovski: "Behind all this – rather as with the erect figure of a skater going at full speed – one always sensed the day, preceding all his other days, when he had taken an extraordinary flying start which had set him off so straight on his prodigious, effortless course." And in the novel he says of his heroine, Lara: "There is the same ease and harmony in everything she does, as if, way back in her childhood, she had taken a flying start in life and everything had followed of itself, as naturally as a result flows from a cause." The curious thing here is not the repetition as such. Pasternak looked upon *Doctor Zhivago* as his crowning achievement that in a certain sense summed up his life's work; it was hence only natural that it should incorporate the whole of his previous literary and intellectual experience – one finds something similar in Lermontov, Tolstoi and Chekhov. The point of interest is that, after brusquely revising his opinion of Mayakovski in *An Essay in Autobiography*, he was nevertheless reluctant to part with the image he had formed of him at an earlier period, and now transferred his erstwhile enthusiasm for him (as expressed in the description quoted above) to his beloved fictional heroine. But if this remarkably apt and psychologically penetrating description fitted Mayakovski to perfection, it strikes one as a mere rhetorical flourish when applied to Lara, a wholly contrived and artificial figure. The image, superbly fashioned as it is, is vastly impoverished by the fictitious nature of the whole context.

There is a good deal, both in the narrative and in the speeches of the characters, about the blessings of the "daily round" of ordinary life, but in fact there is nothing of this at all in the novel: the details of ordinary, everyday existence are secondary and often imprecise, and worst of all – conventional. It is all rather as in a weak play, devoid of atmosphere and tangible detail.

There is a strange internal contradiction in the novel. Near the beginning the author says through one of his characters that "man does not live in a state of nature, but in history". This is true, but the whole novel is conceived in an unhistorical way – even from the point of view of Pasternak's own understanding of history as the work of solving "the enigma of death, so that death itself may eventually be overcome". The strangely condensed and sometimes unjustifiably sketchy quality of the narrative betrays an inexpert hand – or rather, the hand of one expert in a different genre. Many of the narrative devices are distinctly secondhand – all the endless nocturnal conversations, for instance, or Lara's attempt to shoot Komarovsky, and the way she leaves her husband. This is mere "literature", like almost all the extraordinary sudden encounters and coincidences, culminating in the appearance of Zhivago's daughter at the end.

I believe that Pasternak's mistake was in choosing the wrong form for the major prose work of which he had so much dreamed all his life. Unlike Tolstoi who found a uniquely suitable medium in the long epic novel, or Herzen who created an inimitable form of memoir for himself, Pasternak borrowed something foreign to his own temperament and, instead of becoming one with it, he was only able to fit it very loosely over what he wanted to say, and ended up as the prisoner of it. He probably decided on a novel simply because he wanted to appeal to a much broader and, as it were, more popular readership than he would have done with a volume of personal reflections or reminiscences. I had seen myself how much he longed to reach the largest possible audience – the reason, no doubt, why he spoke of his "envy" for the authors of *Cement* and *The Rout*, and hankered after a success in the theatre. It is a matter of observation that when novelists or story-writers try their hands at drama, they are so keen to master its laws that they often go in for mere staginess or pseudo-theatrical effects. The evolution of Chekhov as a dramatist from *Ivanov* to *The Cherry Orchard* was one of emancipation from the current conventionalities of the stage. But when Pasternak chose the traditional form of the novel as a vehicle for the expression of his most cherished ideas and observations, evidently in the hope of achieving the widest possible impact (playing to the gallery, as it were), he fell prey to a misplaced desire to hold the reader's attention by "telling a story" with readily-understood elements of drama in it.

All the specifically Russian background in the novel is somehow artificially intensified, almost stylized. It is so much the Russia of literary tradition, a Russia as seen at second-hand, that I occasionally had the impression of reading a translated work (particularly in the parts where the effect of a novel is most sought-after). This is how people write and speak about Russia if they see it less through their own eyes than through those of Dostoyevski or Bunin in his later years. This is how we, for our part, often write and speak about foreign countries. It is an almost schematized, very exotic Russia of samovars, religious festivals, Christmas trees, and conversations lasting all night long: a stylized essence of Russia. Is this the reason, perhaps, that the book had such a tremendous success abroad? It came out there at a time when the perennial mystery of the "Russian soul" had been compounded by the enigma of a Bolshevik Russia which had not long before emerged victorious from the most terrible of wars – not to mention the super-enigma of the recently ended reign of Stalin. Received abroad as something that offered a key to these mysteries, it does not in fact throw real light on any of them. There is no proper or complete treatment of any aspect of Russian life as it was during the period covered by the novel. On the whole it is a very maladroit and inorganic grafting of the author's sometimes penetrating and often subtle personal reflections onto the crudely constructed framework of a novel à la Dostoyevski.

Pasternak's inadequacy as a novelist is sometimes such that one can only stand in amazement before the numerous commonplaces of a type never encountered in his poetry, and you even wonder whether they can possibly have been written by the same hand. But then, in other passages – mostly the lyrical or descriptive digressions – you suddenly see the unmistakeable touch of Pasternak the poet: "The spring breeze came in through the open window, tasting faintly of newly cut white bread." From this phrase alone you recognize the author. Or: "Outside, the houses and fences huddled closer together in the dusk. The trees advanced out of the depth of the gardens into the light of the oil-lamps shining from the windows." And: "If a charred log prevents the fire from drawing properly, I run out with it smoking in my hand and fling it as far as possible into the snow. It flies through the air like a torch, throwing sparks and lighting up the white square lawns of the sleeping park, and then buries itself, hissing, in a snowdrift." Or: "The lime trees were in blossom. Their scent was everywhere at once, as though outdistancing the travellers on their journey north, like a rumour which flew to every siding, signal-box, half-way house, awaiting them on their arrival . . ."

There are many such passages, but so much else that is forced, overdrawn or derivative. How true he is to his own excellent taste in places like these, and how it deserts him when he strays into unfamiliar territory!

A similar (and even more tragic) example of the failure of a great artist to prove himself outside his proper sphere was that of Scriabin, whose attempts at writing poetry were published after his death by Gershenzon in a volume of the *Russian Propylaea*. Uniquely original and profound as a composer, Scriabin the poet was revealed as an inept and jejune imitator of Symbolist commonplaces. Yet he is known to have attached enormous importance to his excursions into verse, sincerely regarding himself as a pioneer blazing new trails. I must qualify this: Pasternak *did* write excellent prose – but prose of a different kind. The traditional novel, sad to say, defeated him.

Once, in Chistopol, Pasternak and I had talked about Leonov's strange remark that he regarded Pushkin's *The Captain's Daughter* as the supreme achievement of Russian literature, and Pasternak had given me a subtle explanation of this contradiction between what Leonov admired and the way he actually wrote himself. But in the writing of *Doctor Zhivago* almost the same kind of thing happened to Pasternak. Seeking to emulate Tolstoi and Chekhov, he wound up as an imitator of Dostoyevski. With his gift for the subjective monologue, he was unable to master the novel of ideas, with its clash of opposing sides. However, wherever there are descriptive passages in a true "Tolstoyan" spirit, the prose is strong and pure – as for example in the remarkable episode of the Tsar's visit to the front.

I will say nothing of Pasternak's turn towards religion, which came late in life and finds expression in the novel. This is a matter of opinion. Personally I find it strange and I share the view of the young Pasternak who thought that the blossoming of a branch in Kamyshin in May was "more grandiose than Holy Writ".*

One could say a good deal more about this extraordinary book, so full of internal contradictions, so uneven and unnecessarily complex. As an act of courage on the author's part it is heroic, and its moral premises are impeccable, but the literary result is debatable. As regards the aspects of it that made such an impression in some circles in the West – and disturbed many of us here – I need only quote what the author himself says about one of the novel's main characters:* "He took offence at things at which one doesn't take offence. He sulked at the course of events. He quarrelled with history. To this day he is trying to get even with it . . ." It could not be better put.

I began to write these notes out of an undying feeling of affection and reverence for Pasternak, out of gratitude to him. I would forfeit my right to these feelings and be unworthy of his friendliness towards me, if I were to be dishonest as regards *Doctor Zhivago*. Our love for the chosen few must not be servile: this is one of the great lessons he taught us himself.

There was talk about the award of the Nobel Prize to Pasternak already in 1957 and by 1958 it seemed a foregone conclusion. I no longer remember what fed these rumours – perhaps it was reports on foreign radio-stations. At the end of October, the rumour turned into a fact.

It became known in Moscow, I believe, on October 24. (The day before we had the first snowfall of winter, but it quickly thawed.)

The very next day *Literary Gazette* (whose editors had evidently prepared for the event) published a very long letter to Pasternak from the editorial board of *Novy Mir*.

It took up almost two pages of the newspaper and explained the reasons for the journal's rejection of the novel. It was accompanied by an editorial of exceptional harshness. On the 26th there was a lengthy article by D. Zaslavski entitled "On a Literary Weed" (the "weed" being Pasternak). It was now that his name became known to everyone.

Two days before Yesenin's death, when Aseyev had a conversation with him about, among other things, what it meant to be a poet, Yesenin defended the right of a poet to write popular lyrics for the consumption of the general public. Aseyev wrote down his remarks word for word: "If you don't write lyrics, no one will ever know you: for every pound of flour, you need a pound of dung. Without fame, you won't get anywhere, try as hard as you like – no one will listen. You'll just go through life like a Pasternak!..." Aseyev adds: "This is exactly what he said, I remember very clearly." (*S. A. Yesenin*. Memoirs edited by I. Yevdokimov. State Publishing House, Moscow 1926, page 194.) It is interesting that in a later reminiscence of Yesenin, Aseyev gives a very different version of this conversation without any mention of Pasternak's name.) For Yesenin, in the middle of the twenties, Pasternak's name was thus synonymous with total obscurity so far as the public as a whole was concerned. Little changed in the following thirty years: Pasternak's name remained unknown outside the narrow literary world, student circles and some part of the intelligentsia. But during these two days, October 25 and 26, his name became known literally to everybody.

During the night of the 26th there was another snowfall and it stayed on the ground almost till the evening. I was sitting in a barber's shop on Arbat Square that afternoon when I heard Zaslavski's article being read out over the radio. Everybody listened in silence – a sullen kind of silence, I would say. Only one chirpy workman started talking about all the money Pasternak would get, but nobody encouraged him to go on. I knew that cheap tittle-tattle of this kind would be much harder for Pasternak to bear than

166

all the official fulminations. I had felt very depressed all day, but this silence in the barber's shop cheered me up.

For the next few days a little snow lingered on the still-green grass of Moscow's public gardens – a very beautiful sight. Then there was another thaw, the winter retreated and autumn returned with glorious sunny weather.

The campaign against Pasternak gathered momentum. On October 27, the presidium of the Union of Soviet Writers expelled him from the organization. On October 31, a meeting of the Moscow branch of the Union ratified this decision and passed a resolution demanding that Pasternak be stripped of Soviet citizenship.

All this is still fresh in our minds. Needless to say, many of the people who joined in the attack on Pasternak were merely putting it on. This was the last relapse into that state of utter terror which was still with us from the days of Stalin. I remember a conversation I had during the concerted attack against Zoshchenko in 1946, when I asked a certain writer who took part in it how he could reconcile his present violent remarks with the praise he had only recently lavished on Zoshchenko. He replied in ringing tones: "If I have to choose between Zoshchenko and my country, I choose my country . . ." This formula, so magnificently frank in its demagogy, could easily have been used by many of Pasternak's accusers, but the simple truth is that they were once again gripped by the sickening, clammy feeling of dread which they knew so well . . .

Two well-known writers happened at the time to be staying in the writers' rest-home in Yalta.* Geographical distance thus prevented them from being present at the meetings of the Writers' Union in Moscow, but fearing that silence might reflect unfavourably upon them, they both hastened to dash off violent articles against Pasternak for publication in the local Yalta newspaper. One of them was an eminent poet of whom Pasternak had several times spoken well, and who had once publicly described him as his teacher. The other writer was someone who had virtually been his friend, who had known him well for many years and had often written warmly about him in his books.

Misha Svetlov, who was living out at Peredelkino that autumn, told me how one dark evening some local hooligans and drunks threw stones at Pasternak's windows. They also shouted anti-Semitic remarks. Misha felt nothing but sympathy for Pasternak and deplored the way he had been so wilfully misunderstood. I couldn't sleep that night, thinking of Pasternak's house plunged in darkness, the windows with the drawn curtains and the locked gate . . .

Pasternak has himself described his state of mind during those days in his poem "Nobel Prize", which begins:

> I am caught like a beast at bay.
> Somewhere are people, freedom, light,
> But I hear only the yelping of the pack,
> No way out is left for me.*

At the theatres (the Moscow Arts, and the Maly) where plays translated by him were running, his name was removed from the posters.

This "sign of the times" (to use a favourite phrase of our critics) immediately stirred tragic memories from the past. It looked as if we could expect something even more terrible and irreparable. Everybody rushed to read the newspapers in the mornings, and sat glued to their radios in the evenings. There was no shortage of news at that moment: A Vatican conclave elected Cardinal Angelo Roncalli as the new Pope John XXIII. Academician Tamm and two other Soviet scientists also received the Nobel Prize. Sergei Radlov died in Riga, and Academician Orbeli in Leningrad. But nobody spoke of anyone but Pasternak. This is how he became the object of the kind of fame once dreamed of by Yesenin.

The days got shorter and darker. I was filled with misgivings not only out of pity for Pasternak (and a feeling of shame for many others), but also because the whole business had a nasty ring of the black Stalin years about it.

On the last day of the month we heard about Pasternak's

telegram to the Nobel Prize committee. The text (never published here) read: "In view of the significance attached to your award by the society in which I live, I am obliged to renounce the undeserved distinction conferred upon me. I beg you not to take my voluntary renunciation amiss." At the same time he sent his well-known letter to Khrushchev* – it was published in the newspapers on November 2 – asking to be allowed to keep his Soviet citizenship. The reply came in the form of a TASS announcement which said that Pasternak was free to act as he wished. Although Kochetov once more denounced him in print as a "turncoat" and Mikhalkov published some sneering doggerel about him, the campaign now slowly but steadily died down.

After this, Pasternak began to suffer more and more from ill-health. He started on the play, of which I have spoken earlier, and conducted an enormous correspondence replying to all the letters that came pouring in from all over the world.

The hard-working recluse who never read the newspapers had become almost overnight a sensational, much sought-after figure. He was pursued by foreign journalists who hung on his every word. Those who managed to gain entrance to his house described his writing table, his wicker chair, bookshelves, and neckties. Their stories – not always free of fantasy – were published in the world's newspapers. As a result, the postman brought ever larger piles of letters to his door. This is how he wrote about it himself:

> Hairfine from tree to tree
> The evening shadows trail.
> A forest road: the postwoman
> Meets me with my mail . . .
> Mountains and lakes, islands
> And continents unfold:
> How many reviews, discussions,
> Children, young people, old . . .
> As for you, stamp collectors,

What wealth to pick and choose
If you could stand a moment
In my unlucky shoes . . .†*

In 1959 and the first part of 1960 I spent very little time in
Moscow and know hardly anything about his life at this
time. Now and again I heard rumours about his health.
The ominous word "cancer" was mentioned.

During all these difficult times he had a close and faithful
friend in his neighbour, Vsevolod Ivanov, from whom I
heard that he was genuinely aghast at the element of modish-
ness in the success of the novel by which he set such store.
He wrote several letters to translators abroad, begging them
not to bring out versions of his early poems, but to no avail.
In the meantime, he wanted to finish his play about a serf
actress, and dreamed of writing a new prose work in which
he hoped to show "what can be achieved if the style is so
reticent that it becomes, as it were, the actual language of
the things and situations described". He also proposed to
turn his notes about his work as a translator into a major
essay on Shakespeare and Goethe. (Note of a conversation
with Ivanov, February 1961.)

I do not know the exact date of the poem "Fame's not
a pretty sight".* It was included by Pasternak in a new
volume of poems under the title *When the Weather Clears* in
which he intended to gather together all the poems written
between 1956 and 1960. But even if this one was composed
before the Nobel Prize and all the bitter ordeals of the
autumn and winter of 1958, it nevertheless seems like a
response to thoughts occasioned by the change which then
came about in his relations with the outside world and his
own country: as often in the case of a true poet, the lyrical
response may anticipate rather than follow an event. And
besides, Pasternak had known all along what to expect and
what it would be like, except perhaps for a few details:

† Translation by Michael Harari.

Success is not your aim,
Nor noise, but gift of self.
Shameful to be a legend
On all lips, and an empty name.
To win before you die,
The friendship of the spaces
And hear the future speak
Means living a life and not a lie . . .
Merge into privacy
Like landscape into fog,
Blinding the passer-by
With absolute nothingness to see.
Though other pairs of feet
Will tread your living footsteps
It's not for you to settle
What's victory and what's defeat.
And yet you must defend
Each inch of your position,
To be alive, only
Alive, only alive to the end.†

† Translation by Michael Harari.

5

And now I come to that day which stands out so extraordinarily in my memory, down to the minutest detail: June 2, 1960, the day of Boris Pasternak's funeral.

Not long before, I had gone up to Leningrad, aware that he was very ill. I spent the evening and sat up part of the night before my departure with an old comrade from the forced labour camp, E. L. Shternberg. A professor of history and expert on the Middle East, Shternberg was one of Yakov Elsberg's "god-children".* He dearly loved Pasternak's poetry and in remote Obozerka,* near the White Sea, we had often played a game of seeing which of us could remember most of him off by heart. And that evening, in one of the Kislov side streets,* we of course talked about Pasternak and his illness. There had just been a rumour that he was a little better.

In Leningrad I opened each new number of *Literary Gazette* with great trepidation, always fearing to see a black-edged announcement in the usual place for such things at the bottom right-hand corner of the back page.

It so happened that I actually returned to Moscow on June 2nd. As I left the station I bought a copy of *Literary Gazette* and put it in my coat pocket without looking at it. After attending to some business I had in a couple of places, I went home. The moment I opened the door, the telephone rang. It was some friends who had called to tell me that Shternberg had died suddenly during the night of May 31, and that his cremation had taken place an hour ago. Before

I could ask any questions, they went on to tell me that in twenty minutes' time they were going to Peredelkino for the funeral of Pasternak who had also died that same night. I said I would come with them. For a while I stood there dazed. Then, almost without thinking, I pulled *Literary Gazette* from my raincoat pocket and read the famous notice about the funeral of "*Litfund* member" Boris Pasternak . . .*

It was very hot that morning, and the sky was clear, but by midday some light, wispy clouds appeared. There were four of us in the car. On the way I was given details about the final stages of his illness and his last moments. He had asked repeatedly for the window to be opened − although it was in fact open, and this of course was already being interpreted in a symbolic sense, like Goethe's "Mehr Licht!", or Pushkin's farewell to his book-shelves. There is nothing to be done about such things. Any trifle may be raised to the level of myth, or − as Pasternak himself had once put it − the smallest detail "grows in meaning at a farewell". The humble northern cloudberry is for ever associated with Pushkin's dying moments in my mind.* Pasternak, they told me, had spoken of the window when he was already semi-conscious. A little while before, coming to while being given an injection, he had supposedly said in anguish: "Now why do you torment me? I am going to die in any case . . ." He may have said something quite different, or something else as well, or nothing at all − though this phrase has an authentic ring about it and I could almost hear him saying it. It was too early yet for a "cloudberry" to be chosen from all the true or apocryphal versions of his last words and enshrined in legend. The myth had not yet solidified.

The road wound up and down hill like a grey ribbon. Here was the intersection with another road forking off to the left into a dense gloomy forest and leading straight to the house which had once been Stalin's country retreat. Over seven years had gone by since his death, but everything round here still seemed heavy with dark mysteries, even though the house had long since been turned into a children's sanatorium. Every time they passed this sinister junction, Muscovites could still not help recalling the grim-faced police on motor-cycles who always used to keep watch here – if "police" is the right name for them. But this was now all past history. We hurtled by at fifty miles an hour and on past the green woods and gardens, already in full bloom, of the countryside outside Moscow. It was a beautiful summer's day. Now there was a new turning, and yet another – and soon we were in the village: here was the bridge, the lake bounded by black posts with white stripes and bushy willow-trees (it was here that three years ago I had gone walking with him), and the surviving part of the old grounds with the limes and larches . . .

At the last turn-off but one there was a policeman standing in the middle of the road. There had never been anything like this before. He stopped our car and asked sternly where we were going. The driver of the car, to be on the safe side and hoping not to draw attention to the purpose of our journey, gave a house near Pasternak's as our destination. Seeing through the trick and not in the least put out by it, the policeman answered imperturbably that if we were on our way to Pasternak's funeral, we should leave our car here. There were already a couple of dozen cars or so parked along the right-hand side of the road – among them some bearing diplomatic licence plates, as one of my fellow-passengers observed. (Another of them noted that, judging by the pips on his shoulders, the policeman had the rank of major. I couldn't say – I was past noticing such things by now.) We walked into Pavlenko Street. Pasternak's house was the second or third from the corner. We went through the wide-open gate. There were already quite a few people in the garden and I saw some familiar faces. The sounds of a piano came through the open windows. White and purple lilacs were in full bloom in the garden, and slender apple-trees stood in their pink-and-white finery.

We went through into the room where Pasternak's body lay. He was in a black suit and white shirt. The coffin was half-covered by the flowers strewn over it. His face was sallow, very gaunt, and handsome.

Three large wreaths had been placed against the wall at the foot of the coffin. The ribbons were all creased, but one could make out individual words: "To my friend, the poet . . ." Later I was told that two of them were from Vsevolod Ivanov and Kornei Chukovski, and the third, a smaller one, from our precious *Litfund*.

From the next room the sound of the piano came loudly. Maria Yudina, Sviatoslav Richter and Andrei Volkonski were taking it in turns to play without interruption.

We went slowly past the coffin, not taking our eyes off the handsome face. This time I was not struck, as always before, at how young he looked. But neither was it the face of an old man. I had not seen much of him after his hair had gone grey and had not managed to get used to the sharp contrast it made with his youthful features. I still remembered the very first thin threads of silver, hardly noticeable as yet, but already very becoming.

I paused at the doorway and looked back. We went through the porch and out of the house at the other side.

The garden was gradually filling up with people, although there were still over two hours to go before the coffin was due to be taken out for the burial. I saw Konstantin Paustovski, Lev Slavin, Veniamin Kaverin, and Sokolov-Nikitov, now growing old . . . People were standing around in small groups, talking quietly. One or two made jokes, but it did not shock: there was nothing downcast or mournful about the general mood, which was, rather, almost festive in its solemnity. The garden was a riot of blossom under the high June sky . . .

More and more people kept coming in through the wide-open gates: well-known faces of writers, composers and artists; and young people, many young people.

By now there were also a good many foreign journalists, photographers and newsreel men in the garden. They were calm and business-like – mostly strapping fellows with bow ties and often accompanied by female interpreters in glasses; they did their job impassively, without fuss. Someone pointed Henry Shapiro out to me, the Moscow correspondent of the largest American news agency, a short, tubby man dressed in a noticeably casual fashion.

They were all clicking away with their cameras, taking particularly frequent shots of Paustovski. I was sorry I hadn't brought my "Zenith" with me.

Nearly everybody brought flowers. The rooms inside were piled high with them.

Suddenly I heard a voice quietly calling me by name. It was S., an old friend from the labour camp. He stood before me, sweating, his nose peeling, with some books under one arm and a raincoat over the other. After his "rehabilitation" he had gone to live in a small town in Belorussia and was taking a course as an external student at the Institute of Librarianship in Moscow. He had arrived there that morning to sit an examination, but learning from other students about Pasternak's funeral, he had immediately rushed to the Kiev station just as he was, with his books and examination notes. He told me that by the ticket office for the suburban trains somebody had put up a large, hand-written notice about the funeral, with directions as to which train to take and how to find the house. I recalled that S. wrote poetry in the camp and used to read it to me in a whisper at night, when everybody in the barracks was asleep. He had been released a year after me, and this was our first meeting since 1954.

This was not the only chance encounter that day with an old friend from the camp. I also ran into the brilliant young literary scholar and specialist on the epic folk poems of the East, Mel-y.* He had already, since his release, managed to bring out an important scholarly work. (In the camp he worked as a lowly clerk in the medical section.)

But there was nothing all that accidental about such meetings in this place on that particular day. We all remembered the lines: "My soul, you are in mourning / for all those close to me / turned into a burial vault / for all my martyred friends . . ."*

I have already described how warmly Pasternak embraced me when we first met after my release. I had sometimes felt the urge to write to him from *there*, but was afraid it might compromise him. I know that others did write, and that he replied, even if he did not know them: the poets V.S. and K.B. still have letters he wrote to them while they were in labour camps. But no more need be said about this: it is sufficient to re-read "My soul . . ."

More and more people arrived. It would be quite impossible to name all the close and distant acquaintances, and all the other people I knew only by sight, now thronging round the house. I can mention only a few, more or less at random, leaving out others not by design, but because there were so many. I could see Boris Livanov, who was rehearsing the role of Hamlet at the Arts Theatre in Pasternak's translation of the play. Then there was the philosopher and historian, Professor V. Asmus, a friend of Pasternak for very many years; the translator and artist Wilhelm Levik; two women poets – the elderly Vera Zviagintseva, and Maria Petrovykh (with whom Pasternak had been friendly in Chistopol); the author of a history of Renaissance Literature, Pinski (also one of Elsberg's "god-children"); Sukhomlin, a former Social-Revolutionary and now an emigré, who had come to Moscow as a correspondent of *Libération*, and Natalia Stoliarova, another old resident of Paris, and former prisoner in a labour camp; P. A. Markov, V. Liubimova, A. Granberg, Alexander Fevralski, E. M. Golysheva, Nikolai Otten, Nikolai Chukovski, Lyuba Ehrenburg, Vsevolod Ivanov. Among the crowd one could occasionally glimpse the pale face of Elie Nusinov. There were the literary scholars and critics Lev Kopelev, Andrei Sinyavski, Arkadi Belinkov; the young poets Vladimir Kornilov, Naum Korzhavin, Bulat Okudzhava; and the young prose-writers Yuri Kazakov and Boris Balter.

And many, many others: young people in spectacles –

students of the Film Institute, or of architecture, perhaps; budding musicians with faces familiar from competitions at the Conservatory; grey-haired women, their eyes swollen with tears (I overheard one of them talking about Pasternak and referring to him as "Boria"* – what was she to him, I wondered?); a thin youth with protruding ears, a future physicist or poet, or astronomer, perhaps. He would remember this day for the rest of his life.

Every generation, and every professional group of the Moscow intelligentsia was represented. Some people were very conspicuous by their absence: Fedin, Leonov and Nikolai Aseyev (who had known Pasternak from the days of his youth). Another well-known poet, it was said, had been on the bottle for the past three days, telling his drinking companions that all people were swine. Fedin, we heard, had pleaded illness and was sitting it out in his house nearby, ordering the curtains to be drawn so that the murmur of voices from the funeral crowd would be muffled.

I kept looking for my friend I., who also lived nearby. He had always been proud of having at least a nodding acquaintance with Pasternak, and was genuinely indignant at the treatment meted out to him. At last I saw his wife. Catching my enquiring glance, she came up and began to explain quickly, as though apologizing, that I. had been "summoned to town" that morning, but would otherwise have come without fail. She made the point too insistently for it not to ring false.

For some time I had noticed another well-known writer, K., standing with his wife on the other side of the garden fence, but not coming in. They seemed to be arguing – she loudly, and he rather sheepishly. Finally, with a wave of her hand, she came in through the gate, while he stayed outside. The supineness caused by many years of fear could be read in his embarrassed expression as plainly as in a book. Not everybody had the amenable conscience of I. with his carefully prepared alibi. Willy-nilly I began to think what a wide range of different types of cowardice there are: from the staid, almost decorous variety to the hysterical, breast-beating kind; from the shamelessly unconcealed to the hypocritically furtive.

And there was yet another ugly mark that day. Very noticeable among the crowd were certain individuals who were looking round them with more than just idle curiosity. They were eavesdropping on conversations and also clicking away with cameras. I picked out one of them in particular and watched him for quite a while. He pretended to be waiting to get into the house with the rest of the crowd, but he was just marking time, his eyes constantly darting from side to side. His open-necked sports shirt, low forehead and distinctive expression made him unmistakeable. Types such as this – as well as the foreign journalists who had also come only to do their job – were the sole alien element in the crowd which, with all its diversity, was united in its shared feelings.

People were still arriving in large numbers. It was remarkable how orderly this crowd was, with no attempt to organize or shepherd it. Without anyone telling them what to do, not hurrying or pushing, people filed through the house past the coffin – though, admittedly, one occasionally saw the indispensable, good-hearted and discreet Ari Davydovich Ratnitski moving among them in his usual inconspicuous fashion. There was one other representative of *Litfund*, with a scared, peevish expression on his face.

The crowd now filled the whole of the garden between the fence and the house. Many others were waiting outside. How many were there altogether? Two or three thousand, or four? It was hard to say, but it was certainly a matter of several thousand, and scarcely less than three. As we were driving there, I had worried in case it turned out to be rather poorly attended and pathetic. Who could have expected so many, when nobody *had* to come just for form's sake, by way of duty, as is so often the case. For everybody present it was a day of enormous importance – and this fact itself turned it into yet another triumph for Pasternak.

179

Somebody pointed out Olga Ivinskaya to me. She was sitting on a bench by the house with bowed head, listening to something Paustovski was telling her. She was the subject of Pasternak's last lyrics and I couldn't help studying her features, looking for the likeness to the portrait drawn in all the memorable poems about her.

We stood for several more hours in the festively blossoming garden while new groups of people still continued to come in through the gate with flowers in their hands.

A few more hours went by like this – I don't remember exactly how many. All the time there was only one topic of conversation: Pasternak.

But now the way into the room with the coffin was barred for twenty minutes to everyone except the family. Ivinskaya remained in the garden. After a while she climbed up on the bench and looked through the window. The newspaper men were delighted and a dozen cameras began to whirr and click.

The windows were flung open and armfuls of flowers were passed out to the crowd. There were so many flowers that it took quite a time: they sailed slowly overhead back to those who had brought them. When the procession at last moved off, nearly everyone was carrying flowers again.

Somebody handed the wreaths through the door, and the lid of the coffin. And then the coffin itself.

I felt a lump in the throat.

My friends and I moved on ahead, so as not to be at the back of the procession.

Some enterprising Americans had managed to improvise a kind of platform from crates and boards outside the gate for their cameramen, who had already taken up position on it.

The graveyard was six or seven hundred metres away by the road, but much nearer if one took a short-cut over a potato field. We went across the field and got there twenty minutes before the procession.

A truck was standing ready to take the coffin, but the young people carrying it would not allow this and bore it all the way themselves.

The place chosen for the burial could not have been better or more beautiful: it was open to all sides on a hillock with three pine trees, in sight of the house where the poet had lived the second half of his life.

The crowd already waiting here seemed even larger than in the garden. The procession with the coffin arrived. Before setting it down on the ground, next to the grave, the pall-bearers for some reason lifted it up above the crowd and for the last time I saw the face, gaunt and magnificent, of Boris Leonidovich Pasternak.

I was about ten paces away from the grave, but had no wish to push my way closer, as the journalists were doing. Even here they had managed to find, or had brought with them, some wooden boxes to make a stand for themselves. Henry Shapiro elbowed his way past me.

The burial ceremony began. The first to speak was Asmus. It was no easy thing to do, but he managed it superbly. I do not remember very well what he said, but not a single word seemed out of place.

The elocutionist Golubentsev recited "Oh, had I known it would be thus . . ."*

And then I heard another, unfamiliar, voice reciting in a modern, unaffected intonation the poem "Hamlet", still not published here,* but widely known. It would have been hard to choose better. At the last lines a murmur went through the crowd. The atmosphere immediately became a little tense, but the same voice which had announced the beginning of the ceremony (I could not see who it was because of all the people in front of me) now hastened to call an end to it. The murmurs grew louder, and there were some shouts of protest, among which somebody immediately piped up in a saccharine voice about how the poet would soon turn into dew, and suchlike mawkish mystical nonsense. This had no sooner finished than somebody else started up

181

in a hoarse and hardly sober voice, demanding to know in the name of the workers of Peredelkino (*workers* in Peredelkino?) why it was that "Pasternak was never printed" and declaring that he had "loved the workers". This already had a whiff of political provocation about it, but the omnipresent Ari Davydovich quietly gave the word, and we heard the order: "One, two . . . ready!" They were lowering the coffin into the grave. More shouts were heard:

"Goodbye, the greatest of all!"

"Goodbye, Boris Leonidovich!"

"Goodbye! . . ."

There was dead silence for a moment and then we heard the clods of earth thudding down on the coffin lid.

It was still hot, but the sky was now hazed over by a thin covering of cloud.

A portable movie camera was whirring away. Somebody began to sob: it was all too much for the nerves. But on the whole there were few tears that day – only as the coffin was being carried out of the house, and now. In general the mood had been solemn and uplifted.

But the moment the coffin was covered over, loud arguments broke out among several groups of young people, and others began to recite poetry. Somebody was looking for Validol, saying that Maria Petrovykh had been taken ill.

We walked slowly back to our car. I had a branch of white lilac from the coffin in my hands.

We drove home in silence. None of us wanted to talk: each of us had his own thoughts, which he was loath to dissipate in conversation, hoping to keep them for ever.

It was eight o'clock by the time we reached Moscow. The hot day had now given way to a sultry evening.

This was my last day with Pasternak.

An old book much admired by our ancestors, the famous *Oracle* by Baltasar Gracián y Morales,* tells us that a man's highest quality, apart from intelligence and other natural gifts, is "openness and an honourable and liberal independence of spirit".

Zagoryanskaya, September 1963
Komarovo, December 1964.

NOTES AND COMMENTS

Some of these notes are intended for the general reader and others more particularly for specialists with a knowledge of Russian. It is hoped that the several lengthy comments on passages where further elucidation seemed appropriate may be of interest to both. The Russian title, or first line, of poems quoted in the text has been given to make it easier to identify and locate the originals: most of these (except for a few fragments hitherto unpublished elsewhere, and a number of the *Doctor Zhivago* poems) may be found in the one-volume Soviet edition of Pasternak's poetry published in Moscow in 1965 (*Boris Pasternak: Stikhotvorenia i poemy*) with an introductory article by Andrei Sinyavski; the *Doctor Zhivago* poems may be found in the Western Russian-language editions of the novel, and several late poems still not published in the Soviet Union are available in the bilingual edition: *Poems, 1955–1959* (English versions by Michael Harari), London, 1960.

Basic information about the many persons mentioned in the text, except in a few cases where it was impossible to trace them in the available sources, is given in the alphabetically arranged Biographical Guide.

page 32 "The roofs of towns you pass . . ." (*Kryshi gorodov dorogoi . . .*): the last stanza of the poem "The Artist" (*Khudozhnik*), first published in 1936.

page 34 Shigalyov: character in Dostoyevski's *The Possessed*, a nihilist who dreams of an ideal state of the future in which society will be held together by mutual denunciation and spying. In his *An Essay in Autobiography* (London, 1959, page 92) Pasternak uses the term *shigalyovshchina* ("Shigalyovism") to describe the Great Purge of 1937.

"Pushkin plenum": a full session of the board of the Union of Writers held in connection with the hundredth anniversary of Pushkin's death, which fell in 1937.

. . . André Gide's *Retour de l'URSS*: after an initial period of enthusiasm for the Soviet Union Gide expressed his disillusionment in this book which caused great indignation in Soviet official circles.

page 35 MIFLI: Moscow Institute of Philosophy, Literature and Art, which has become legendary for the relative independence of spirit of some of its students. (Solzhenitsyn was an external student of it in the late thirties.) It was merged with Moscow University during the war.

. . . Two wars: the first was the "Winter War" with Finland (1939–40) which, though short, was costly in human life for the Soviet Union.

page 36 FOSP: "Federation of Associations of Soviet Writers", predecessor of the Union of Soviet Writers, and housed in the mansion on Vorovski Street (formerly Povarskaya Street) in Central Moscow, traditionally supposed to have been the home of the Rostovs in Tolstoi's *War and Peace*.

Spektorski: long poem which in some respects anticipates *Doctor Zhivago*.

"Accustomed to picking out . . ." (*Privykshi vykovyrivat . . .*): first lines of the Introduction to *Spektorski*.

"Space sleeps . . ." (*Prostranstvo spit . . .*): line in stanza 11 of Part 1 of *Spektorski*.

page 37 *Ogoniok* (*The Flame*): popular illustrated weekly (founded in 1923 by Mikhail Koltsov, q.v. in the Biographical Guide). It also put out mass editions of Russian and foreign classics, and contemporary writers.

The Rift (*Razryv*): a cycle of nine poems written in 1918 and first published in 1922.

"Marburg": written in 1915 and first published in 1917.

Pasternak attended courses in philosophy at Marburg in 1912.

Klyazma: tributary of the Moscow river.

Neskuchny Sad: park in central Moscow, near the river. (Now a continuation of Gorki Park.)

page 38 "A lilac branch rainsodden like a sparrow" (*namokshaya vorobyshkom sirenevaya vetv*); "Raindrops weighty as cufflinks" (*U kapeltyazh est zaponok*): lines from the poem *Ty v vetre . . .*, 1922.

"An evening empty as an interrupted tale" (*Vecher pust kak prervanny rasskaz*): from *Vesna*, 1918.

Second Birth (*Vtoroye rozhdenie*): major cycle of lyrics dated 1930–31.

My Sister Life (*Sestra moya zhizn*) and *Above the Barriers* (*Poverkh baryerov*): volumes of poetry published in 1922 and 1917 respectively.

page 39 *Zvezda* (*Star*): monthly literary journal.

Safe Conduct (*Okhrannaya Gramota*), published in 1931, is an autobiographical account of the author's early life.

. . . Georgian poets: e.g. Titian Tabidze and Paolo Yashvili, who were his personal friends and fell victim to the purges in 1937. See *An Essay in Autobiography*, London 1959 (and New York under the title *I Remember*) and *Letters to Georgian Friends*, London and New York, 1968.

page 40 "A High Illness" (*Vysokaya bolezn*), a long poem which appeared between 1924 and 1928. Pasternak was present when Lenin addressed the 9th Congress of Soviets in 1921 and was profoundly impressed by him. The line "A genius comes . . ." (*Predvestyem lgot prikhodit genii . . .*) is the last in the poem and has been restored in the one-volume edition of 1965.

. . . Stalin's telephone call: for the full story of this, see Nadezhda Mandelstam, *Hope Against Hope*, London and New York, 1970. The main purpose of the call was to inform Pasternak that the death sentence on Mandelstam for writing a poem denouncing Stalin had been commuted to exile in a provincial town.

Culture and Life (*Kultura i zhizn*): a weekly newspaper which served as the Party's main mouthpiece during the post-war purges of the Soviet intelligentsia. The attack on Pasternak (March 22, 1947) was signed by Alexei Surkov (q.v. in the Biographical Guide) and was hence somewhat less ominous than an unsigned editorial would have been: it was meant to intimidate Pasternak, rather than give the signal for his destruction.

Znamia (*The Banner*): a monthly literary journal. The publication here of a selection of the "Zhivago" poems (the religious ones and "Hamlet" were not included) with a note saying they were part of a forthcoming novel, was one of the most notable signs of the "thaw" in the year after Stalin's death.

. . . A large new collection of Pasternak's verse: this edition, which had already been set up in proof in 1957, was cancelled because of the Nobel Prize "scandal" and never published. However, copies of the proofs survived and were used in the preparation of the important 1965 edition (where there are frequent references to the "Proofs" [*Verstka*] – a bibliographical curiosity no doubt unique of its kind). The autobiographical sketch written by Pasternak as an introduction to this never-published volume appeared in English translation in 1959 and only years later in Moscow in the original (see note to page 151).

page 41 *On Early Trains* (*Na rannikh poezdakh*); *Earth's Space* (*Zemnoi Prostor*): collections published in 1943 and 1945; they include poems written after 1936, and wartime poems. The poem to Marina Tsvetayeva (*Pamyati Mariny Tsvetayevy*) was not published until 1965.

Chistopol: on the river Kama, about 650 km east of Moscow.

V.U.O.A.P.: *Vsesoyuznoye upravlenie po okhrane avtorskikh prav* (All-Union Commission for the Protection of Authors' Rights), a dependency of the Union of Soviet Writers which handles authors' royalties and provides certain secretarial facilities, etc.

page 44 Peredelkino: writers' colony in a village 20 km south-west of Moscow, where Pasternak had a house from 1936 until his death.

page 49 *Litfund* (*Litfond*, from *literaturny fond*, "literary fund") : an organization (affiliated since 1934 to the Union of Soviet Writers) which ministers to the material needs of writers – giving them grants, finding accommodation, even arranging their funerals. It is financed by compulsory contributions from the Soviet publishing houses. Persons expelled from the Union of Writers sometimes remain members of *Litfund* – as happened in the case of Pasternak in 1958.

page 51 Alma-Ata: capital of the Central Asian Soviet republic of Kazakhstan.

Sons of Glory (*Pitomtsy slavy*): title of Gladkov's *Long, Long Ago* as staged by the Leningrad Comedy Theatre in 1941.

page 53 Yasnaya Polyana: Leo Tolstoi's country house and estate south of Moscow, preserved as a museum. The Germans deliberately set fire to it during their retreat, but the house was saved from destruction by local people.

makhorka: coarse tobacco.

page 54 . . . new play . . . with Arbuzov: *The Immortal One* which had its première in the Red Army Theatre, 1943.

page 56 Skalozub: figure in Griboyedov's play *Woe from Wit* (1822–24), a martinet.

page 58 Pasternak wrote relatively few lyrics after *Second Birth* until the eve of the war. The reference to work "involving public affairs" may apply to a small cycle of poems in the mid-thirties (notably those published in *Izvestia* on New Year's Day, 1936) in which he made a last attempt to come to terms with the era – after which he was almost literally struck dumb by the horrors of Stalinism, and took refuge in translation until the war. His verse on wartime themes had still not been published at the time of this conversation.

page 60 Lavrushinski Street: street in Central Moscow where Pasternak had an apartment in a 12-storey block built specially for Soviet writers.

page 74 Polytechnic: The Polytechnic Museum in Moscow,

whose large auditorium is often used for public lectures and poetry readings.

page 76 . . . Romeo's final lines: "Thou desperate pilot, now at once run on / The dashing rocks thy seasick weary bark". In the short poem he wrote before his suicide Mayakovski spoke of "love's boat" having been dashed against ordinary life.

page 77 "I feel guilty at not having tried to dissuade her . . .": Pasternak met Tsvetayeva during his visit to Paris in 1936, when he was at the last minute included in the Soviet delegation to a World Congress of Writers in Defence of Peace. For an account of this meeting, see Pasternak's *An Essay in Autobiography* (page 107).

page 78 "a giant of the pre-Christian era of human history": the same idea appears in *Doctor Zhivago*: ". . . history as we know it now began with Christ . . . There was no history in this sense in the classical world. There you had blood and beastliness and cruelty and pockmarked Caligulas untouched by the suspicion that any man who enslaves others is inevitably second-rate . . ." (English translation, page 18).

page 79 *Somebody Else's Baby* (*Chuzhoi rebionok*): a farce by Vasili Vasilyevich Shkvarkin (1894–1967), a popular playwright who enjoyed a great vogue in the thirties.

page 80 . . . Incident with Pasternak: the incident already described on page 45.

The Precipice: stage version of the novel of this name by Goncharov.

page 81 "Salieri complex": reference to Pushkin's drama in verse about Salieri's jealousy of Mozart (1830).

page 82 GPU, NKVD: earlier names for the Soviet secret police (now KGB).

LEF: "Left Front", the post-Revolutionary association of Russian Futurists, in which Mayakovski was the dominant figure. It published a journal under the same name.

page 83 *avoska*: string shopping bag popularly known thus from the colloquial adverb *avos*, used to express optimistic expectation that something might be achieved or obtained.

page 84 "Tiutchev's famous aphorism": "A thought uttered is a lie" (*Silentium!*, 1833).

page 87 Khlestakov: hero of Gogol's *Inspector-General*.
The Rout (1927), novel by Fadeyev; *Cement* (1925), novel by Fyodor Gladkov. Both are considered orthodox classics of Soviet literature.

page 89 *The Fruits of Enlightenment*: a comedy by Leo Tolstoi (1891) satirizing contemporary society.

page 92 . . . a drama in prose: the idea of this projected play is briefly described on page 102.

page 95 Kazan: the capital of the region, and a short journey from Chistopol. The author was flying on from here to Sverdlovsk, which is some 480 km to the east, in the Urals (the Red Army Theatre had been evacuated there from Moscow).
. . . Pasternak himself had brought it: there is no explanation of why the author did not take the note and manuscript with him to Kazan, instead of having them brought by Arbuzov.

page 96 . . . forces encircled near Kharkov: a sudden German counter-attack at the end of May and the beginning of June 1942, led to a severe defeat for the Soviet South-West army group.

page 97 All-Russian Theatre Association (VTO): an organization founded in 1883 which looks after the material needs of actors, arranges public lectures on the theatre, etc.

page 102 . . . my hand-written copy of "The Old Park" contained four stanzas missing from the version as published: the "missing" stanzas are quoted in the Russian text, but are omitted in this translation. The same stanzas (with a few trifling differences) are reproduced, from a manuscript in the State archives, in the notes to the poem in the 1965 edition. "The Old Park" (*Stary Park*), written in 1941, describes the thoughts of the young Samarin as he lies, his foot amputated, in his ancestral home in Peredelkino, to which he has been brought back by the chance of war. If he survives, he will write a play about the war. The stanzas omitted from the published version (such as the line "all his dreams were of the theatre") do indeed read like a reflection of Pasternak's own theatrical ambitions in the first two years of the war. The Samarin mentioned in the poem cannot be Dmitri Samarin, the grandson of the Slavophile and Pasternak's friend from university days, because this Samarin died of typhus at the end of the twenties. (There is a description of him in Pasternak's *An Essay in Autobiography* – pages 77–9 of the English edition – from which it is clear, as Gladkov mentions on page 148, that he must have been to some extent the prototype of Yuri Zhivago in the novel.) The Samarin in the poem is described as a *great*-grandson of the Slavophile, and could thus have been a son or nephew of Dmitri. The Slavophile Yuri Fyodorovich Samarin (1819– 74) is buried on his former family estate at Peredelkino.

page 108 *Mission to Moscow*: a flattering picture of Soviet life based on the book by Joseph Davies (1876–1958), U.S. Ambassador to the Soviet Union, 1937–38.

page 114 "Nightglow" (*Zarevo*): the text of this unfinished work (including several passages quoted by Gladkov from his manuscript copy, but omitted in the translation) is to be found in the 1965 edition of Pasternak's poetry. The "Introduction" of 52 lines appeared in *Pravda* in October, 1943. "Chapter One", consisting of 140 lines and dated October, 1943, was published for the first time only in the 1965 edition.

As Gladkov says, one does not need to be a Cuvier (the French palaeontologist who reconstructed pre-historic animals from their skeletal remains) to see that the poem, if ever completed, would have been very disturbing from the point of view of ideological orthodoxy – soon, with victory, to be re-established with greater severity than ever before. It is indeed somewhat astonishing that the passage with the reference to Priestley and Hemingway should have been published even in the edition of 1965. The "Introduction" also contains undertones which would have made its appearance in *Pravda* quite unthinkable three or four years later – though there is nothing particularly insidious about it (this would have been foreign to Pasternak), since it only reflects more or less openly the general, unconcealed expectation of the post-Stalingrad period that the enormous sacrifices of the Soviet people would be rewarded with internal relaxation after victory. It was even, perhaps, official policy – for obvious tactical reasons – not to discourage this mood, just as nothing much was done to counter a widespread belief among the peasants that the hated collective farm system might be abandoned after the war. The title, "Nightglow", refers to the spectacular gun salutes in Moscow to the ever more frequent and decisive victories of the Red Army. By the autumn of 1943 the night sky of Moscow was almost continually lit up by them. In the poem's Introduction, where they are described with Pasternakian vividness, a Red Army soldier returning home on leave sees them as he approaches the city – a city now "as bright as the future". The "Nightglow", both in reality and in the poem's imagery, was too obviously a presage of better times even to be allegorical. (In his usual guileless manner, Pasternak announces in the second part that he is writing "without allegory" when he identifies the "Nightglow" of his title with its bearer, the returning Red Army soldier.) There are many suggestive phrases which speak not only of the expectation of freedom, but of the certainty that it would be demanded as of right by the returning victors before whom darkness (not only in the sense of war and invasion) is already retreating symbolically in the sky over Moscow: the soldier swears like a Zaporozhian Cossack (always in Russia the historical personification of freedom at its most unbridled); those who fought at the front have been "reborn" in war; there will be the "novelty of the people's role" (*novizna narodnoi roli* – which immediately to a Russian ear suggests the rhyming word *voli* – "freedom" or "will", and hence an association with the Populist "People's Will" [*Narodnaya Volia*] which fought to overthrow the tyranny of the Tsar in the 1870's). Even the most slow-witted Soviet censor must have seen here an alarming vista of implied historical references – beginning with the Decembrist uprising against Nicholas I in 1825 after the victory over Napoleon. The "First Chapter", long unpublished, goes even further. Apart from the opening passage which explicitly contrasts the truthfulness of Russian literature in the past with its falsity and venality in the Soviet present, there is a frank description of what the returning soldier finds at home: black marketeers (his wife has evidently taken one for a lover), selfishness and petty concern for one's own well-being, etc. If the poem had been completed, this contrast between the idealism of the returning soldier and the moral inertia on the home front would inevitably have led up to radical implications of a much broader nature.

. . . Fadeyev had been advising Soviet writers to model themselves on Turgenev rather than Chekhov: Chekhov's ostensibly dispassionate way of describing the moral and other failings of his contemporaries was clearly not a suitable one for Soviet writers in the post-war period when literature was required to gloss over the harsh realities and project a fanciful picture of a happy and abundant life after victory (for which sole credit was given to the Party and Stalin personally).

page 117 *Stone*: see note in the Biographical Guide on Mandelstam.

page 119 *A Twin in the Clouds* (*Bliznets v tuchakh*): Pasternak's first collection of lyrics, published in 1914. It was followed by *Above the Barriers* (*Poverkh baryerov*) containing verse written in 1914–16 (published in 1917), and *My Sister Life* (*Sestra moya zhizn*), poems written in the summer of 1917 and published in 1922. The latter was the one that firmly established Pasternak's reputation as a major poet. The "long poems on the revolution of 1905" are "Nineteen Five" (*Deviatsot piaty god*), 1925–26, and "Lieutenant Schmidt", 1926–27.

page 120 the Polyanka: a district in central Moscow.

. . . an excerpt from his narrative poem would shortly be appearing in *Pravda*: the Introduction of "Nightglow" mentioned above. It was published on October 15, 1943.

page 121 "The Death of a Sapper" etc. (*Smert sapiora, Presledovanie, Razvedchiki, Zima nachinayetsa* – later title: *Zima priblizhayetsa* – *Neogliadnost*) were all written at the end of 1941 and appeared together as a cycle of poems on the war in *On Early Trains*.

. . . small volume of his selected poems: *Izbrannye stikhi i poemy*.

Kolyma: a vast and desolate area along the river Kolyma in the Soviet Far North-East, notorious for its forced labour camps under Stalin.

page 122 "Waltz with ghosts" (*Vals s chertovshchinoi*): the poem actually appears in *Earth's Space* under the title "At Christmas" (*Na Rozhdestve*) and this was its first publication.

page 124 Pasternak's "impromptu epigram" and his "birthday message" to Kruchenykh have never been published elsewhere.

"Fame's not a pretty sight" (*Byt znamenitym nekrasivo*): first published in 1956, in *Znamia*, and then included in Pasternak's last collection *When the Weather Clears* (*Kogda razgulyayetsa*), verse of 1956–59.

page 125 "My relations with certain people in the West": the significance of this is that the wider and more spontaneous human contacts which the freer atmosphere of wartime made possible had brought home to him that he was not just an isolated intellectual (the whole purpose and effect of Stalinist terror was to make every individual imagine despairingly that he was the *only* one left to think his own thoughts), but that his feelings and views were shared by many of his compatriots, and would receive their assent if he could find a way of conveying them. At the same time, thanks to the still very limited but enormously important contact with the outside world brought about by the wartime alliance between the Soviet Union and the Western powers, Pasternak would have understood that he was well enough known and appreciated abroad as one of Russia's greatest living poets to be able to count on moral support there in the event of his speaking out in some way. In a word, he no longer felt hopelessly cut off from the world outside, as well as from his own countrymen. In the late war years and in the year or so afterwards (before Stalin re-imposed full-scale terror in 1946, brutally stamping out the shortlived wartime sense of solidarity among his subjects, and sealing off the country even more effectively than ever), Pasternak not only received news of his family in Oxford, but also learned of translations of his work and articles about him published in England and America during the war. A few direct personal encounters with members of the small foreign colony in wartime Moscow (diplomats, journalists, etc.) – among whom were some with a special concern for and knowledge of Russian literature – confirmed him in his new realization of the esteem in which he was held. To at least one of his Western friends just after the end of the war, he confided that he intended to "speak out". Apart from writing *Doctor Zhivago* (at a time when it was highly dangerous to commit anything to paper, let alone show it to others – as he did) he came very close to a direct public expression of his attitude on the occasion described in the Introduction.

page 126 Mokhovaya: broad thoroughfare in Central Moscow between the Kremlin and the old University building.

... several extracts in *Literary Gazette*: one of the many prose fragments published in the twenties and thirties which contain incidents or names later incorporated in *Doctor Zhivago*.

Volkhonka: street in central Moscow.

page 127 ... a great new love: Olga Vsevolodovna Ivinskaya (q.v. in the Biographical Guide). Many of the poems in the *Doctor Zhivago* cycle and in *When the Weather Clears* are devoted to her.

page 128 ... article on his translations of Shakespeare: This eventually appeared in print in 1956, in *Literaturnaya Moskva*

(*Literary Moscow*), volume 1.

The article on Blok never appears to have been completed, or at least has never been published.

The critic T.: the following passage almost certainly refers to Anatoli Tarasenkov (q.v. in the Biographical Guide).

page 129 *Bezbozhnik* (*The Atheist*): newspaper edited by Emelyan Yaroslavski. It ceased publication in July, 1941.

page 131 ... article in *Culture and Life*: see note to page 40.

Bolshevik (later renamed *Kommunist*): monthly theoretical journal of the Soviet Communist Party, in which major ideological pronouncements were customarily made. Stalin's reply to Colonel E. Razin (a professor of military history) in *Bolshevik*, no. 3, 1947, was directed against Clausewitz's theory of war, despite the fact that Lenin had on occasion quoted him with approval.

... The reaffirmation of the cult of Ivan the Terrible: this "cult" of Ivan the Terrible and of other Russian autocrats (notably Peter the Great) had begun already before the war, and was a consequence of Stalin's decision in the mid-thirties to attempt to identify himself in the public mind with those past rulers of Russia who had applied ruthless repression at home, supposedly as an essential condition for the active pursuit of Russia's defence against foreign enemies or territorial expansion at their expense. The second part of Eisenstein's film *Ivan the Terrible* (the first part was made in 1942) aroused Stalin's acute displeasure because Eisenstein, whether unwittingly or not, created the impression that Ivan's special security force, the *oprichnina*, was a predecessor of the modern kind of totalitarian one (which indeed it was in some ways). The film was condemned violently in a special Party decree of September 4, 1946. Stalin was so incensed that he virtually destroyed the Soviet film industry, which only began to recover years after his death. In order to fill the gap created by the closing down of almost all Soviet film studios, several anti-British and anti-American films (*The Last Round* – about the fixing of boxing matches in New York by a Jewish promoter; *The Sinking of the Titanic*, and *The School of Hatred* – on English tyranny in Ireland) made by the Nazis and seized in Germany at the end of the war, were dubbed in Russian and shown to Soviet audiences as "new foreign films". The second part of *Ivan the Terrible* was publicly screened in Russia only after Stalin's death. The Party decree condemning Eisenstein's film was one of a series between the end of 1946 and 1948. The net effect of these attacks on chosen scapegoats (Akhmatova, Zoshchenko and Pasternak in literature; Muradeli, Shostakovich, Khachaturyan in music, etc.) was to reduce the Soviet intelligentsia to a state of terrorized conformity from which it began to recover only long after Stalin's death.

page 132 . . . the edition of his selected verse . . . was destroyed: this volume had actually been announced for publication by the "Soviet Writer" (*Sovietski Pisatel*) Publishing House. During the anti-Semitic campaign against "homeless cosmopolitans" which began at the end of 1948, the director of this publishing house, Levin, was denounced in the press for having "had the impudence" to attempt to re-publish work by Pasternak.

"contract for *Faust*": this translation, the only complete one in Soviet times, was published in 1953.

page 133 Alexandrovski Garden: a park, one section of which runs between the Kremlin wall and the Moscow River.

page 134 "the mulatto Pushkin": Pushkin's great-grandfather on his mother's side was an African named Hannibal who was presented to Peter the Great by the Sultan of Turkey.

page 135 Natalia Nikolayevna: Natalia Nikolayevna Goncharova, Pushkin's wife, whom he married in 1831. The suggestion is that if she had agreed to retire to Pushkin's country estate at Mikhailovskoye, Pushkin might not have become enmeshed in the social intrigues at the court in St Petersburg, which led to his tragic and premature death in a duel six years later.

page 137 *A Dreary Story* (*Skuchnaya istoriya*): one of Chekhov's best known longer stories (1889).

page 138 "Monument" (*Ya pamyatnik vozdvig* . . .): celebrated poem, written a year before his death, in which Pushkin speaks of his assured posthumous fame.

page 141 "Winter Night", "March", "In Holy Week", etc.: with the exception of the first two, none of these poems from the *Doctor Zhivago* cycle has ever been published in the Soviet Union.

page 142 "There are words whose meaning . . ." (*Yest rechi – znachenye* . . .): the first stanza of this short poem reads in full: "There are words whose meaning / is dark or trivial, / yet which stir the soul / when you hear them."

"unheard-of simplicity" (*neslykhannaya prostota*): a line from Pasternak's long poem "Waves" (*Volny*), part of the collection *Second Birth*, 1930–31. He speaks here of the "unheard-of simplicity" into which every great poet must fall at last, "as though into a heresy". The "merciless retribution" it brought down on Pasternak's head was, of course, the persecution of him after the publication abroad of *Doctor Zhivago*.

page 145 ". . . 'still uncorrected'": Stalin's concentration camps were officially called "corrective labour camps".

. . . poems in *Znamia*: see note to page 40.

. . . the first verse of his . . . to be published in all these years: i.e. the first original work of Pasternak's to appear in the Soviet Union since the collection *Earth's Space* in 1945.

page 146 "Bacchanalia": a long poem written after the première of Schiller's *Maria Stuart* in 1957. "Bacchanalia" forms part of *When the Weather Clears*. When Pasternak says here that he still has "no luck" with the theatre, he presumably refers to his failure to complete any original play of his own. His translation of *Maria Stuart* enjoyed a great success on the Soviet stage.

page 147 . . . long play about a serf actress: i.e. *The Blind Beauty* (*Slepaya krasavitsa*), never completed and published abroad in English and Russian as a fragment only in 1969. A few months later in the same year, the text was also published in the Soviet literary journal *Prostor*.

. . . the meeting of Moscow writers: on October 31, 1958. A number of well-known Soviet writers spoke out against Pasternak at this meeting.

page 151 *An Essay in Autobiography*: The third volume of *Literary Moscow* (*Literaturnaya Moskva*) never appeared. (The first two volumes of this almanac both came out in 1956, and represented a concerted attempt on the part of a group of liberal writers to establish a more independent publication; this seemed possible in the favourable atmosphere after Khrushchev's denunciation of Stalin at the 20th Party Congress, but the venture foundered during the reaction in the wake of the Hungarian uprising in November 1956.) *An Essay in Autobiography* was originally written by Pasternak as an introduction to a collection of his poems which was set up in type in 1957, but never published because of the "scandal" over *Doctor Zhivago*. It first appeared abroad in English translation (London and New York, 1959), and only subsequently, with some cuts, in Moscow (*Novy Mir*, 1967, under the title *Liudi i polozheniya. Avtobiographicheski ocherk*).

page 152 . . . V. Vishnevski's vulgar and offensive toast: It has not been possible to obtain any details of the incident. For Vishnevski, see the Biographical Guide.

page 153 the manuscript of the novel was given by Pasternak to Feltrinelli with the knowledge of *Novy Mir* and *Goslitizdat*: the account in this paragraph of the circumstances in which Feltrinelli received the manuscript is not accurate. The completed manuscript had first been submitted by Pasternak in the summer of 1954 to *Novy Mir*, *Goslitizdat* and to *Znamia* (which had earlier, in April 1954, published some of the verse with a note by the author saying that the novel of which it formed part would be completed shortly). Then, for two years, nothing happened, except that false rumours were spread abroad to the effect that Pasternak had not in fact completed the novel, and the announcement of its forthcoming publication by *Znamia* had hence been premature. At the same time vague promises were made to

Pasternak that some part of the novel *might* be published. It was quite clear, however, that the original promise to publish (made in the euphoria of the first "thaw" after Stalin's death in the spring of 1954) would not be kept. In the spring of 1956 – no doubt encouraged by Khrushchev's denunciation of Stalin at the Party Congress in February of the same year – Pasternak handed a copy of the novel to a young Italian communist, Sergio D'Angelo, who had recently arrived in Moscow to work as an announcer in the Italian section of Moscow Radio (and who had been asked by the Milan Communist publisher, Giangiacomo Feltrinelli, to act unofficially as his representative in Moscow). Pasternak gave D'Angelo the manuscript *without* the knowledge of *Novy Mir* and *Goslitizdat*, and without permission from the Soviet authorities. It was only *after* the latter had learned of Pasternak's action that a renewed promise was made to publish the novel and an editor even appointed to handle it. However, it soon became clear that this new promise was only a manoeuvre to gain time in the hope of recovering the manuscript from Feltrinelli and frustrating publication abroad. Feltrinelli refused to give it up, despite strong pressure from Moscow and the Italian Party authorities, and the novel was duly published in the Italian translation in 1958. In the early autumn of 1956, Pasternak availed himself of an unexpected opportunity to send a second copy of the novel abroad, evidently to assure foreign publication in the event that Feltrinelli failed to bring it out for some reason or other.

Giangiacomo Feltrinelli (1926–72) was a Communist millionaire whose publishing house specialized in the publication of works on the history of the labour movement. In the sixties he became involved with extreme left wing activities. He was killed in March 1972 while apparently attempting to blow up an electric pylon near Milan. (For the background to the bizarre circumstances of his death, see "Feltrinelli" by Luigi Barzini, *Encounter*, July 1972.)

page 155 . . . decision to pulp the volume of his poetry: see note to page 132.

. . . major poem by Pasternak: i.e. the poem entitled "Gethsemane" in the *Doctor Zhivago* cycle.

page 156 *One Day in the Life of Ivan Denisovich* and *Matryona's Home*: these works by Alexander Solzhenitsyn were published in *Novy Mir* in November, 1962 and January, 1963 respectively.

"But the book of life . . .": the 12th stanza of "Gethsemane".

page 157 "Exact to the hundredth . . .": from the poem "Fulfilment" (*Vse sbylos*), in the collection *When the Weather Clears*.

page 158 . . . the young procurator: i.e. official of the "procuracy" (*prokuratura*) – the judicial authority in the Soviet Union theoretically responsible for seeing that the law is correctly applied, and also for initiating prosecutions. After Stalin's death it was the procuracy which conducted the formal process of "rehabilitating" persons who had been unjustly sentenced.

page 165 . . . the blossoming of a branch in Kamyshin in May was "more grandiose than Holy Writ": the reference is to a stanza of the poem "My Sister Life . . ." in the collection of the same name first published in 1922. There is a confusion here, evidently due to the lines in question having been misremembered. Pasternak speaks not of the "blossoming" (*rastsvetanye*) of a branch in Kamyshin, but of the "timetable" (*raspisanye*) of the trains on the *branch-line* to Kamyshin (a town in the Volga region). The comparison of a time-table to Holy Writ clearly has no significance for Pasternak's earlier attitude to religion.

. . . one of the novel's main characters: Antipov-Strelnikov, the first husband of Lara and a revolutionary. The words quoted (page 397 of the English translation of *Doctor Zhivago*, Fontana edition) are actually spoken by Lara.

page 167 . . . Two well-known writers: Ilya Selvinski and Victor Shklovski (q.v. in the Biographical Guide).

page 168 "I am caught like a beast at bay . . ." (*Ya popal, kak zver v zagone* . . .): this poem, needless to say, has never been published in the Soviet Union. It received wide publicity in the Western press at the time.

page 169 . . . well-known letter to Khrushchev: the text of this and other relevant documents in the "Pasternak affair" may be found in Robert Conquest's *Courage of Genius* (London, 1961).

page 170 "Hairfine from tree to tree . . ." (*Teni vechera volosa tonshe*): from the poem entitled "God's World" (*Bozhi mir*), and the last in the cycle *When the Weather Clears*.

"Fame's not a pretty sight . . ." (*Byt znamenitym nekrasivo* . . .): first published in 1956.

page 172 . . . Yakov Elsberg's "god-children": i.e. people denounced by Elsberg (q.v. in the Biographical Guide).

Obozerka: forced labour camp about 100 km south of Archangel, where the author served his sentence.

. . . the Kislov side streets: series of side streets in an old part of Moscow, near the Conservatory.

page 173 "*Litfund* member" Boris Pasternak . . .: though he had been expelled from the Union of Writers, Pasternak remained a member of the *Litfund*, and this is how he was described in the meagre notice of his funeral (for which *Litfund* made the arrangements). There was no obituary in the Soviet press of one of Russia's greatest poets.

. . . humble northern cloudberry: Pushkin asked for cloud-berries as he lay dying after his fatal duel.

page 176 Mel-y: evidently Meletinski (q.v. in the Biographical Guide).

page 177 "My soul, you are in mourning . . ." (*Dusha moya, pechalnitsa* . . .): included in *When the Weather Clears*, but never published in the Soviet Union (the Russian text and full English translation may be found in *Boris Pasternak, Poems 1955–59*, London, 1960 – a bilingual edition with trans-lations by Michael Harari).

page 178 "Boria": an intimate, diminutive form of "Boris".

page 181 "Oh, had I known it would be thus . . ." (*O, znal by ya, chto tak byvayet* . . .): poem by Pasternak first published in 1932, as part of the cycle *Second Birth*.

. . . "Hamlet", still not published here: It is true that the poem has not been published officially as an original work of Pasternak in the Soviet Union, but since Gladkov wrote this it has been quoted in full by Andrei Voznesenski in an article on Pasternak's translations in the monthly journal *Foreign Literature (Inostrannaya Literatura)*, January, 1968. In this context it was evidently taken by the censor as a translation from Shakespeare!

page 182 *The Oracle (El Oráculo manual y arte de prudencia, 1647)*: a book of maxims which was translated into Russian in the eighteenth century.

BIOGRAPHICAL GUIDE TO PERSONS
MENTIONED IN THE TEXT

AFINOGENOV, Alexander Nikolayevich (1904–41): leading Soviet playwright; killed in air-raid on Moscow.

AGRANOV, Yakov Savlovich (1893–1938): Cheka investigator in the Kronstadt mutiny and other uprisings against the Soviet régime in its early years; the creator and chief of *Litkontrol*, a GPU department for surveillance over writers. As deputy head of the NKVD under Yagoda and Yezhov, he was active in the preparation of the Moscow show trials of 1937–38. (Cheka-GPU-NKVD: successive names of the Soviet secret police, now KGB.) He was arrested and shot in 1939 – presumably because of his association with Yezhov, who fell into disfavour with Stalin once the great purges were over. Gladkov gives Agranov's first name as Jan. He appears to be mistaken in giving the date of his death as 1937.

AKHMATOVA, Anna Andreyevna (1889–1966): great Soviet poet who was condemned to silence for most of the Soviet era. Her first husband, Nikolai Gumilev, was shot as a "counter-revolutionary" in 1921. Her second husband and son were imprisoned during the terror of the thirties (and her son a second time after the war). She was allowed to appear in print again for a brief interlude beginning in 1940 (*From Six Books*, *Iz shesti knig*), and with several patriotic wartime poems, such as "Courage" (*Muzhestvo*), in 1942. In 1946 she was the chief target, together with Zoshchenko (q.v.), of a violent official attack which signalled the beginning of the renewed campaign of terror against the intelligentsia.

ANTOKOLSKI, Pavel Grigoryevich (1896–   ); poet.

APLETIN, M. (dates unknown): editor and critic.

APUKHTIN, Alexei Nikolayevich (1840–93): poet whose work sometimes has a Gypsy intonation. He was a friend of Tchaikovsky who put some of his poems to music.

ARBUZOV, Alexei Nikolayevich (1908–   ): popular Soviet playwright; co-author, with Gladkov, of *The Immortal One* (1942).

ARSKI, Pavel Alexandrovich (1886–   ): poet, prose-writer and playwright.

ASEYEV, Nikolai Nikolayevich (1889–1963): Futurist poet and associate of Mayakovski, to whom he dedicated a long poem, "Mayakovski Begins" (*Mayakovski nachinayetsa*), 1940.

ASMUS, Valentin Ferdinandovich (1894–1975): philosopher and logician; close friend of Pasternak.

BABEL, Isaak Emmanuilovich (1894–1941?): outstanding Russian-Jewish short-story writer, author of *Red Cavalry* (1923). He disappeared after his arrest in 1939, and although he has been posthumously "rehabilitated", the date and circumstances of his death remain obscure.

BAGRITSKI, Vsevolod Eduardovich (1922–42): poet, son of Eduard Bagritski (1895–1934), a major poet of the twentiest

BAKHMETYEV, Vladimir Matveyevich (1885–   ): novelis. and story writer.

BAKHTIN, Mikhail Mikhailovich (1895–1975): literary scholar; author of *Problems of Dostoyevski's Art* (*Problemy tvorchestva Dostoyevskogo*), first ed. 1927.

BALTER, Boris Isaakovich (1919–74): prose-writer. A disciple of Paustovski (q.v.).

BARATYNSKI (or BORATYNSKI), Evgeni Abramovich (1800–44): the most outstanding of the poets among Pushkin's exact contemporaries.

BEDNY, Demyan (1883–1945): versifier of great vigour noted for his anti-religious satires.

BELINKOV, Arkadi Victorovich (1921–70): literary scholar and critic, graduate of the Gorki Literary Institute and of Moscow University, who was arrested in 1944 for writing and circulating a novel which contained fundamental criticisms of the Soviet régime. He was sentenced to death, but the sentence was commuted to forced labour. After thirteen years in prisons and camps, he was released in 1956. In 1960 he published a lengthy study of the novelist and critic Yuri Tynyanov which caused a great stir among the Soviet reading public by its only very slightly veiled "Aesopian" parallels between the most oppressive periods of pre-revolutionary Russian history and the Soviet era. No such devastating critique of the system had ever been published in the Soviet Union itself. In 1968 Belinkov succeeded in emigrating to the United States, where he taught Russian literature at Yale and other universities. His health had been shattered by his experiences and he died in 1970.

BERIA, Lavrenti Pavlovich (1899–1953): Chief of the Soviet secret police from 1938, in succession to Yezhov (q.v.). Executed after Stalin's death (accused, among other things, of having been a British agent).

BOGDANOVICH, Ippolit Fyodorovich (1744–1803): poet of the generation immediately preceding Pushkin.

BOKOV, Victor Fyodorovich (1914–   ): poet.

BOYADZHIEV, Grigori Neresovich (1909–74): leading authority on the theatre and drama critic.

BRIK, Osip Maximovich (1888–1945): friend and associate of Mayakovski. His wife Lili (Lilia Yuryevna) inspired many of Mayakovski's love poems. Her publication in 1958 of Mayakovski's intimate letters to her provoked sharp criticism in the Soviet press, and ten years later an article in the magazine *Ogoniok* (June, 1968) went so far as to hint that she had indeed helped to lead Mayakovski to suicide, in which the refusal of an exit visa to him was a factor. Lili Brik is the sister of Elsa Triolet (who died in 1970), the wife of the French Communist poet Louis Aragon.

BUKHARIN, Nikolai Ivanovich (1888–1938): Old Bolshevik. After being eliminated from the power struggle towards the end of the twenties, he gradually lost all influence, though as editor of *Izvestia* (1934–37), he was still able to intervene on behalf of persecuted writers – notably Osip Mandelstam, whom, at Pasternak's request, he saved from execution in 1935 by appealing directly to Stalin. His speech at the First Congress of Soviet Writers in 1934 showed concern and understanding for real literary values. Arrested in 1937, he was the principal defendant in the last great Moscow show trial in 1938, at which he was sentenced to be shot.

CHAGIN, Petr Ivanovich (1898–1967): editor and director of several Soviet publishing houses.

CHERKASOV, Nikolai Konstantinovich (1903–66): leading actor who played Ivan the Terrible in the first part of Eisenstein's film. In 1946 (the year in which the second part of the film was denounced) he was awarded the Stalin Prize for this.

CHUKOVSKI, Kornei Ivanovich (1882–1969): eminent Russian man of letters; friend and neighbour of Pasternak. His son, Nikolai Korneyevich (1905–65) was a novelist.

DAVYDOV, Denis Vasilyevich (1784–1839): poet who served in the army most of his life and distinguished himself in the war of 1812 as a partisan leader. He cultivated a distinctive "gay hussar" manner in his lyrics.

DELVIG, Anton Antonovich (1798–1831): poet; contemporary

and friend of Pushkin.

DERMAN, Abram Borisovich (1880–1952): literary scholar and novelist.

DOBRZHANSKAYA, Liubov Ivanovna (1908–): leading actress, associated with the Red Army Theatre since 1934; she played the role of Shura Azarova in Gladkov's *Long, Long Ago*.

DOLMATOVSKI, Evgeni Aronovich (1915–): poet.

DZHAMBUL DZHABAYEV (1846–1945): Kazakh poet.

EHRENBURG, Ilya Grigoryevich (1891–1967): novelist, journalist and poet. His wife Liuba (Liubov Mikhailovna) attended Pasternak's funeral.

EISENSTEIN, Sergei Mikhailovich (1898–1948): famous Soviet film director. The second part of his *Ivan the Terrible* was denounced in a Party decree of September, 1946.

ELSBERG, Yakov Yefimovich (1901–): Soviet literary scholar widely believed to have been a secret police informant who was responsible for the arrest and exile of a number of fellow-writers under Stalin (see Nadezhda Mandelstam, *Hope Abandoned*, page 572).

FADEYEV, Alexander Alexandrovich (1901–56): leading "Socialist Realist" novelist and secretary general of the Union of Soviet Writers 1946–53; committed suicide after Khrushchev's revelations about Stalin. He was a neighbour of Pasternak's in Peredelkino.

FEDIN, Konstantin Alexandrovich (1892–): novelist. From 1959–71 he was first secretary of the Union of Soviet Writers.

FET, Afanasi Afanasyevich (1820–92): lyric poet.

FEVRALSKI, Alexander Vilyamovich (1901–): literary scholar and writer on the theatre.

FLORENSKI, Pavel Alexandrovich (1882–1943): priest and theologian, who was deported to Siberia after the Revolution.

FYODOROV, Nikolai Fyodorovich (1828–1903): influential religious thinker.

GALKIN, Samuil Zalmanovich (1897–1960): poet and playwright in Yiddish and Russian; translator of Pushkin, Shakespeare and Mayakovski into Yiddish. Arrested in 1950 during the campaign against "homeless cosmopolitans", but survived imprisonment and was "rehabilitated" after Stalin's death.

GEKHT, Semion Grigoryevich (1903–63): writer known for his stories and novels on Jewish themes.

GERBEL, Nikolai Vasilyevich (1827–83): poet, translator, and editor of editions of foreign classics (including Shakespeare, 1866–68).

GERSHENZON, Mikhail Osipovich (1869–1925): literary scholar and editor; he published archive and other original material in a series of six volumes entitled *Russian Propylaea* (*Russkie propilei*), 1915–19.

GLEBOV, Anatoli Glebovich (1899–1964): playwright. (He is mentioned in Pasternak's poem "Hasty Lines" [*Speshnye stroki*], 1943, about firewatching shortly after the beginning of the war in Moscow.)

GOLYSHEVA, E. M. (dates unknown): translator from English.

GORCHAKOV, Nikolai Mikhailovich (1898–1958): a producer associated with the Arts Theatre and the Moscow Theatre of Satire. Responsible for the Moscow production of Gladkov's *Long, Long Ago* in the spring of 1942.

GORKI, Maxim (1868–1936): major Russian writer who returned to Russia from emigration in 1929. He died in mysterious circumstances, in July 1936.

GORODETSKI, Sergei Mitrofanovich (1884–1967): minor Acmeist poet.

GRIGORYEV, Apollon Alexandrovich (1822–64): poet and literary critic who was associated in the early 1850s with a conservative journal *Moskovityanin* (*The Muscovite*).

GROSSMAN, Vasili Semionovich (1905–64): novelist best known for his wartime work *The People is Immortal* (1942); an unfinished novel *For Ever Flowing* (*Vse techot*) which severely criticizes the whole of past Soviet policy and Lenin personally, was published abroad in 1970.

GUDZENKO, Semion Petrovich (1922–53): poet; student of MIFLI (Moscow Institute of Philosophy, Literature and Art) just before the war. Most of his work is on wartime themes.

GUDZI, Nikolai Kallinikovich (1887–1964): eminent scholar, best known for his work on ancient Russian literature.

GUÉ (or GE in Russian spelling), Nikolai Nikolayevich (1831–94): painter and friend of Leo Tolstoi (whose portrait he painted). Pasternak describes his childhood recollection of him in *An Essay in Autobiography*.

GUSEV, Victor Mikhailovich (1909–44): poet, song-writer and dramatist whose play in verse *Glory* (*Slava*), 1936, was put on by many Soviet theatres.

HERZEN, Alexander Ivanovich (1812–70): famous Russian publicist and political exile; his *My Past and Thoughts* (*Byloye i dumy*), published in London in 1861, is perhaps the finest piece of memoir literature written in Russian.

HUPPERT, Hugo (1902–   ): Austrian poet and translator of Russian literature who emigrated to the Soviet Union in the thirties.

ILOVAISKI, Serafim Dmitrievich (1904–44): actor associated for most of his career with theatres in Siberia.

ISAKOVSKI, Mikhail Vasilyevich (1900–73): poet.

IVANOV, Vsevolod Viacheslavovich (1895–1963): novelist famous for his colourful stories of the Civil War.

IVINSKAYA, Olga Vsevolodovna (1912–): editor and translator. Pasternak met her in the early post-war years. She served to some extent as the prototype of Lara in *Doctor Zhivago*, and a number of the poems in the novel (as well as others in the last cycle, *When the Weather Clears*,) are addressed to her. After Pasternak's death in 1960, Ivinskaya and her daughter were arrested on a trumped-up charge of currency smuggling and sent to forced labour camps.

KAMENSKI, Vasili Vasilyevich (1884–1961): poet at one time associated with the Futurists.

KAVERIN, Veniamin Alexandrovich (1902–): veteran novelist whose stories published in the years since Stalin's death are largely concerned with the unjust persecution of intellectuals.

KAZAKIEVICH, Emmanuil Genrikhovich (1913–62): novelist; the chief editor of *Literary Moscow* (*Literaturnaya Moskva*) the two volumes of which served as a forum for the liberal writers in 1956. (See note to page 151.) His novel *The Blue Notebook* (1961) aroused some controversy, mainly because of its treatment of the relations between Lenin and Zinovyev.

KAZAKOV, Yuri Pavlovich (1927–): one of the younger prose-writers who came to the fore after Stalin's death.

KHESIN, Grigori Borisovich (dates unknown): head of V.U.O.A.P. (see note to page 41).

KHLEBNIKOV, Velimir (1885–1922): Futurist poet.

KHRENNIKOV, Tikhon Nikolayevich (1913–): composer.

KIROV, Sergei Mironovich (1886–1934): Party leader of Leningrad. His assassination in December 1934, which may have been engineered by Stalin, was used as the excuse for the mass terror that began two years later.

KOCHETOV, Vsevolod Anisimovich (1912–73): novelist and editor of the conservative journal *Oktyabr*; author of works lampooning the liberal intelligentsia in the post-Stalin years; committed suicide in 1973.

KOGAN, Pavel Davydovich (1918–42): promising young poet and graduate of MIFLI (Moscow Institute of Philosophy, Literature and Art), who was killed in action during the war. Some of his work has been published only posthumously, in the late fifties and sixties.

KOLTSOV, Mikhail Yefimovich (1898–1942): journalist famous for his dispatches from Spain during the Civil War; arrested in 1938 and presumed to have died in a forced labour camp.

KOLYCHEV, Osip Yakovlevich (1904–   ): poet and song-writer.

KOPELEV, Lev Zinovyevich (1912–   ): graduate of MIFLI (Moscow Institute of Philosophy, Literature and Art) and specialist in modern Western, particularly German, literature. Kopelev is the prototype of "Rubin" in Solzhenitsyn's *First Circle*. The first part of his account of his years in prison and labour camps has been published in the United States: *Keep for Ever* (*Khranit vechno*), Ann Arbor, 1975.

KORNILOV, Vladimir Nikolayevich (1928–   ): poet and prose-writer; author of *samizdat* novel published in the West.

KORZHAVIN, Naum Moiseyevich (1925–   ): poet; emigrated to the United States in 1974.

KOTOV, Anatoli Konstantinovich (1909–56): literary scholar and editor. Director of the State Publishing House for Literature (*Goslitizdat*) from 1948. He played a "liberal" role after Stalin's death; he was one of the editors of *Literary*

Moscow (see note to page 151).

KOZLOV, Ivan Ivanovich (1779–1840): poet and translator; friend and contemporary of Pushkin.

KRUCHENYKH, Alexei Yeliseyevich (1886–1970): Futurist poet.

KULCHITSKI, Mikhail Valentinovich (1919–43): poet who regarded himself as a disciple of Mayakovski and Pasternak. He was killed in the war.

KUTUZOV, Mikhail Illarionovich (1745–1813): commander of Russian army against Napoleon.

LEITES, Alexander Mikhailovich (1899–   ): literary scholar and critic.

LEONOV, Leonid Maximovich (1899–   ): leading novelist and playwright. His play *The Golden Carriage* was written in 1946 but met with official disapproval (evidently because of its rather abstractly moral tone), and appeared only after Stalin's death in 1955.

LEVIK, Wilhelm Veniaminovich (1907–   ): translator of Western European poetry.

LIFSHITS, Mikhail Alexandrovich (1905–   ): literary critic and specialist in Marxist aesthetics.

LIPKIN, Semion Izrailevich (1911–   ): poet and translator.

LIUBIMOVA, Valentina Alexandrovna (1895–1968): playwright.

LIVANOV, Boris Nikolayevich (1904–72): famous actor.

LUNACHARSKI, Anatoli Vasilyevich (1875–1933): leading Old Bolshevik and writer of great versatility (also translator of Hölderlin, Petöfi and others). As People's Commissar for Enlightenment, he directed Soviet cultural policy and affairs almost until the end of the twenties.

MANDELSTAM, Osip Emilyevich (1892–1938): major Russian poet (of the Acmeist school, like Akhmatova), who was arrested in 1934 for a poem denouncing Stalin and would have been executed but for the pleas on his behalf of Bukharin, Pasternak and others. He was instead exiled to Voronezh (where he wrote a last cycle of poems, *Voronezh Notebooks*). After being allowed to return to Moscow in 1937, he was re-arrested in 1938, and died in a camp near Vladivostok at the end of the year. For the story of his ordeal (as well as of his relations with Pasternak), see the memoirs of his widow: *Hope against Hope* and *Hope Abandoned* (London and New York, 1970 and 1974). Apart from his various books of poetry (such as his first, *Stone*, 1913), he was the author of two prose works: the autobiographical *The Noise of Time* (*Shum vremeni*, 1925) and *The Egyptian Stamp* (*Egipetskaya marka*, 1928).

MARKOV, Pavel Alexandrovich (1897–): leading authority on drama; producer at the Arts Theatre, 1955–62.

MAYAKOVSKI, Vladimir Vladimirovich (1893–1930): leading Soviet poet who committed suicide in 1930. Pasternak and he admired each other as poets, but Mayakovski's "canonization" by Stalin in 1935 ("Mayakovski was and remains the best and most talented poet of our Soviet epoch") led Pasternak to comment, in his *An Essay in Autobiography*: "Mayakovski began to be introduced forcibly, like potatoes under Catherine the Great. This was his second death. He had no hand in it."

MAYOROV, Nikolai Petrovich (1919–42): poet, most of whose work was published only after his death at the front.

MELETINSKI, Yeleazar Moiseyevich (1918–): scholar specializing in the study of folk-lore.

MEYERHOLD. Vsevolod Emilyevich (1874–1940): famous actor and producer, who was arrested in 1939 after publicly refusing to accept the doctrine of "Socialist Realism". He died in prison in 1940 and has been posthumously "rehabilitated". Gladkov's reminiscences of him appeared in various Soviet publications (*Novy Mir*, *Moskva teatralnaya* and *Tarusskie stranitsy*) in 1960–61; for excerpts in English see: *Novy Mir*, *A Selection 1925–1967*, edited with an introduction by Michael Glenny, London, 1972.

MICHURIN, Ivan Vladimirovich (1855–1935): Soviet plant breeder.

MIKHAILOV, Mikhail Illarionovich (1829–65): poet and outstanding translator (of Shakespeare and many other Western writers).

MIKHALKOV, Sergei Vladimirovich (1913–   ): poet and playwright known for his deft adaptability in turning out verse on topics of the moment; he is the author of the words (now in abeyance) to the new Soviet national anthem adopted during the war.

MOROZOV, Mikhail Mikhailovich (1897–1952): leading Shakespeare scholar.

MUNBLIT, Georgi Nikolayevich (1904–   ): critic, scenario-writer and memoirist.

NEMIROVICH-DANCHENKO, Vladimir Ivanovich (1858–1943): great Russian theatre director; founder (together with Stanislavski) of the Moscow Arts Theatre (1898).

NIKITIN, Mikhail Alexandrovich (1902–   ): novelist.

NUSINOV, Ilya Isaakovich (dates unknown; now dead): writer of film scripts (son of following).

NUSINOV, Isaak Markovich (1889–1950): Marxist literary critic and scholar (of Russian, Western and Yiddish literature); arrested during the campaign against "homeless cosmopolitans" in 1949 and died in prison the following year.

OBRADOVICH, Sergei Alexandrovich (1892–1956): proletarian poet.

OKUDZHAVA, Bulat Shalvovich (1924–   ): poet, novelist and writer of popular songs which he sings himself, mostly at semi-private gatherings.

OLESHA, Yuri Pavlovich (1899–1960): novelist and playwright. His novel *Envy* (*Zavist*), 1927, is one of the best to have been published in the Soviet Union in the twenties, and shows a certain ambivalence in the author's attitude to the new régime.

ORBELI, Leon Abgarovich, (1882–1958): Academician; eminent physiologist, once a disciple and collaborator of Pavlov (but in 1950 he was accused of having deviated both from Pavlov's teaching and from Marxism).

ORLOV, Dmitri Nikolayevich (1892–1955): leading actor.

OTTEN, Nikolai Davydovich (1907–   ): writer on the theatre and cinema; joint author, with Gladkov, of a scenario published in *Pages from Tarusa* (of which he was the editor, together with Paustovski, q.v.).

PANFEROV, Fedor Ivanovich (1896–1960): novelist and editor.

PARNAKH, Valentin Yakovlevich (dates unknown): poet who lived in Paris in the twenties, and was an acquaintance of Mandelstam – to whom, judging by Picasso's portrait of him, he bore a striking physical resemblance. (He figures as "Parnok" in Mandelstam's *Egyptian Stamp*.)

PASTERNAK, Leonid Iosifovich (1862–1945): father of Boris Pasternak; painter. He emigrated in 1921 with his wife and two daughters, and eventually settled in Oxford, where he died.

PAUSTOVSKI, Konstantin Georgievich (1892–1968): prose-writer best known for his autobiography (in six parts, 1945–63); one of the editors of *Literary Moscow* (see note to page 151), and of *Pages from Tarusa* (1961), a literary miscellany that also played an important part in the development of the liberal movement among the intelligentsia.

PETROVSKI, Dmitri Vasilyevich (1892–1955): poet and prose-writer.

PETROVYKH, Maria Sergeyevna (1908–): poet and translator; at one time a friend of Osip Mandelstam, who dedicated poems to her.

PIATNITSKI, Mitrofan Efimovich (1864–1927): founder and director of a popular choir.

PINSKI, Leonid Efimovich (1906–): scholar specializing in Western European literature, which he taught for many years at MIFLI (see note to page 35) and Moscow University.

PISMENNY, Alexander Grigoryevich (1909–): novelist and story-writer.

POGODIN, Nikolai Fyodorovich (1900–62): well-known and prolific playwright.

POPOV, Alexei Dmitrievich (1892–1961): eminent Soviet producer who directed the Red (Soviet) Army Theatre from 1935–60. He produced Gladkov's *Long, Long Ago* in 1942 while the theatre was evacuated to Sverdlovsk.

POSTUPALSKI, Igor Stefanovich (1907–): poet and translator.

RADLOV, Sergei Ernestovich (1892–1958): leading Soviet producer (particularly of Shakespeare); once an associate of Meyerhold (q.v.).

RATNITSKI, Ari Davydovich (dates unknown): employee of *Litfund* with special responsibility for funeral arrangements.

RAZIN, E. (dates unknown): see note to page 131.

RICHTER, Sviatoslav Teofilovich (1914–): well-known Soviet pianist.

RUDERMAN, Mikhail Isaakovich (1905–   ): poet.

SADOVSKI, Prov Mikhailovich (1874–1947): theatre director.

SCRIABIN, Alexander Nikolayevich (1872–1915): famous composer. There is a chapter on him in Pasternak's *An Essay in Autobiography*.

SELVINSKI, Ilya Lvovich (1899–1968): poet.

SERAFIMOVICH, Alexander Serafimovich (1863–1949): author of *The Iron Flood*, a famous novel about the Civil War (1924).

SHCHERBAKOV, Alexander Sergeyevich (1901–45): veteran Communist official who was appointed secretary of the Union of Writers in 1934. During the war he was a candidate member of the Politburo with special responsibility for the political control of the army.

SHKLOVSKI, Victor Borisovich (1893–   ): veteran literary scholar and critic. Author of several volumes of memoirs: *Zoo* (1923) and others.

SHOSTAKOVICH, Dmitri Dmitrievich (1906–75): famous Soviet composer.

SHUBIN, Pavel Nikolayevich (1914–51): poet.

SIMONOV, Konstantin Mikhailovich (1915–   ): poet, playwright and novelist. His wartime lyrics, and novel *Days and Nights* (on the battle of Stalingrad) made him for a time one of the most popular Soviet writers. The portrait of Galakhov, the successful Soviet writer in Solzhenitsyn's *The First Circle*, is probably based on Simonov.

SINYAVSKI, Andrei Donatovich (1925–   ): scholar, critic and story-writer. In 1965 he was arrested for publishing work abroad under the pseudonym "Abram Tertz" and sentenced to seven years' forced labour. He was released in 1972 and in the following year emigrated to France, where he now teaches Russian literature at the Sorbonne. He wrote the introduction to the most comprehensive Soviet collection of Pasternak's poetry, published in Moscow in 1965, a few months before his arrest.

SLAVIN, Lev Isayevich (1896–   ): prose-writer and memoirist (e.g. of his friend Isaak Babel).

SLUTSKI, Boris Abramovich (1919–   ): well-known Soviet poet and translator who served at the front during the war. Despite his anti-Stalinist record, he attacked Pasternak at the meeting of the Moscow branch of the Union of Soviet Writers in October, 1958, called to discuss *Doctor Zhivago*.

SOFRONOV, Anatoli Vladimirovich (1911–   ): poet and playwright known for his conservative views. The irony of his wartime encounter with Gladkov, described on page 101, is that Sofronov made one of the most scurrilous speeches denouncing Pasternak at the meeting of the Moscow Writers called on October 31, 1958 to condemn *Doctor Zhivago*.

SOKOLOV-NIKITOV, Ivan Sergeyevich (1892–1975): story-writer.

SOLOGUB, Fyodor (1863–1927): Symbolist poet and novelist; his work is officially regarded as "decadent", but a large collection of his poetry was published in 1975 in Leningrad.

SOLOVIEV, Vladimir Sergeyevich (1853–1900): poet and Christian philosopher.

STAVSKI, Vladimir Petrovich (1900–43): prose-writer. As secretary of the Union of Writers from 1936 he was active in the purges of fellow-writers in the following years.

STOLIAROVA, Natalia Ivanovna (date of birth unknown): the secretary of Ilya Ehrenburg, she spent several years in a forced labour camp after coming to the Soviet Union from Paris in 1934. (For a portrait of her, see Nadezhda Mandelstam, *Hope Abandoned*, chapter 38.)

SUDAKOV, Ilya Yakovlevich (1890–   ): theatre director.

SURKOV, Alexei Alexandrovich (1899–   ): poet; first secretary of the Union of Soviet Writers, 1953–59.

SVETLOV, Mikhail Arkadyevich (1903–64): poet and playwright; author of popular romantic poems.

TABIDZE, Titian Yustinovich (1895–1937): Georgian poet, friend of Pasternak. Died in prison during the terror.

TAMM, Igor Yevgenyevich, (1895–   ): Academician; Soviet physicist and Nobel Prize winner.

TARASENKOV, Anatoli Kuzmich (1909–56): literary scholar and critic. (For a comment on him as a collector of poetry, see Nadezhda Mandelstam *Hope Abandoned*, page 479.)

TIKHONOV, Nikolai Semionovich (1896–   ): poet; secretary of the Union of Writers, 1944–46.

TIUTCHEV, Fyodor Ivanovich (1803–73): lyric poet.

TOLSTOI, Alexei Nikolayevich (1882–1945): novelist and playwright; his play *Ivan the Terrible* (1943) gives a favourable portrait of the Tsar.

TRENEV, Konstantin Andreyevich (1876–1945): story-writer and dramatist, best known for his play about the Civil War, *Liubov Yarovaya* (1926).

TSVETAYEVA, Marina Ivanovna (1892–1941): major Russian poet who emigrated in 1923. She returned to the Soviet Union in 1939 from Paris. Soon afterwards her husband (who had gone back before her) was executed, and their daughter was sent to a camp. At the outbreak of war, she was evacuated to the town of Yelabuga, where in August 1941 she hanged herself. She was a friend of Pasternak, Mandelstam and Akhmatova, and ranks with them in the quality of her poetry. Pasternak dedicated two important poems to her: one in 1929; and another to her memory which he was writing in Chistopol, as he mentioned to Gladkov, but which was published only in 1965.

TUMANSKI, Vasili Ivanovich (1800–60): minor poet who published verse in Pushkin's time.

TVARDOVSKI, Alexander Trifonovich (1910–71): poet and editor (of *Novy Mir*). His *Vasili Terkin* (1941–45), written in a simple but very expressive style, achieved enormous popularity during the war. (A satirical, anti-Stalinist sequel to it, *Vasili Terkin in the Other World*, was published in 1963 by special dispensation of Khrushchev, who was well-disposed to Tvardovski personally.)

UTESOV, Leonid Osipovich (1895–   ): popular singer and jazz musician.

VASILYEV, Pavel Nikolayevich (1910–37): poet who enjoyed considerable popularity in the thirties, arrested in 1937 and died in a camp.

VERTINSKI, Alexander Nikolayevich (1889–1957): popular *chansonnier* who returned to the Soviet Union in 1943, via the Far East, after many years in emigration. His songs were banned as "decadent" in the Soviet Union, but became widely known there from foreign recordings brought home by Red Army men after the war.

VINOKUR, Grigori Osipovich (1896–1947): eminent authority on the Russian language and literature, known particularly for his studies of Pushkin.

VISHNEVSKI, Vsevolod Vitalyevich (1900–51): playwright noted for his pliable treatment of Soviet history.

VOLKONSKI, Andrei Mikhailovich (1933–   ): Russian composer born in Switzerland, a student of Nadia Boulanger in Paris, 1944–7. Moved to the Soviet Union and continued his studies there. Has now re-emigrated to the West.

YAKHONTOV, Vladimir Nikolayevich (1899–1945): prominent Soviet actor associated with the Arts Theatre who was noted for his readings of literary works and for his one-man performances. He committed suicide in 1945.

YAKOVLEVA, Tatyana (1911–   ): White emigrée Russian with whom Mayakovski fell in love at the end of the twenties. He addressed one of his last poems to her. The refusal of a visa to him so that he could visit her in Paris was a factor in his suicide (see note on Brik). She now lives in New York.

YASHVILI, Paolo Dzhibrielevich (1895–1937): Georgian poet and friend of Pasternak. Committed suicide during the terror of 1937.

YAVICH, Avgust Efimovich (1900–   ): novelist.

YESENIN, Sergei Alexandrovich (1895–1925): poet noted for his lyrical descriptions of the Russian countryside. In the twenties, before his suicide in 1925, his popularity was rivalled only by that of Mayakovski.

YEZHOV, Nikolai Ivanovich (1894–1939?): chief of the NKVD (secret police), 1936–38, when he was responsible for carrying out Stalin's Great Purge; he was later made the scapegoat for its "excesses", and probably executed in 1939.

YUDINA, Maria Veniaminovna (1899–1970): eminent Soviet pianist and professor at the Moscow Conservatory.

ZASLAVSKI, David Iosifovich (1880–1965): journalist.

ZENKEVICH, Mikhail Alexandrovich (1891–1973): Acmeist poet, associate of Akhmatova and Gumilev before the Revolution; translator of poetry from English and other languages.

ZOSHCHENKO, Mikhail Mikhailovich (1895–1958): story-writer very popular in the twenties and thirties for his wistfully humorous portrayal of everyday Soviet life. On August 14, 1946 he was denounced, together with Akhmatova, in an official Party decree. Both were expelled from the Union of Soviet Writers.

ZVIAGINTSEVA, Vera Klavdievna (1894–   ): poet and translator.